BY RAM CHARAN

"I write books for the use of practitioners."
—Ram Charan

The Amazon Management System
(co-author, bestseller)

*Execution: The Discipline of Getting
Things Done* (co-author, bestseller)

*Confronting Reality: Doing What
Matters to Get Things Right*
(co-author, bestseller)

*The Attacker's Advantage: Turning
Uncertainty into Breakthrough
Opportunities* (bestseller)

*What the CEO Wants You to Know:
How Your Company Really Works*

*Global Tilt: Leading Your Business
Through the Great Economic Power Shift*

*The Game Changer: How You Can
Drive Revenue and Profit Growth
with Innovation* (co-author)

*Leadership in the Era of Economic Un-
certainty: The New Rules for Getting
Things Done in Difficult Times*

*Know-How: The 8 Skills That Separate
People Who Perform from
Those Who Don't*

*Leaders at All Levels: Deepening Your
Talent Pool to Solve the Succession Crisis*

*Profitable Growth Is Everyone's Business:
10 Tools You Can Use Monday Morning*

*Every Business Is a Growth Business:
How Your Company Can Prosper Year
After Year* (co-author)

*What the Customer Wants You to Know:
How Everybody Needs to Think
Differently About Sales*

*Verizon Untethered: An Insider's Story of
Innovation and Disruption* (contributor)

*Strategic Management: A Casebook
in Business Policy and Planning*
(contributor)

Action, Urgency, Excellence (customized
book for EDS Corporation)

Business Acumen (customized book for
Ford Motor Company)

Solid Line, Dotted Line, Bottom Line
(customized book for Gateway)

*Boards That Lead: When to Take Charge,
When to Partner, and When to Stay Out
of the Way* (co-author)

*Owning Up: The 14 Questions Every
Board Member Needs to Ask*

*Boards That Deliver: Advancing
Corporate Governance from Compliance
to Competitive Advantage*

*Boards at Work: How Corporate Boards
Create Competitive Advantage*

*E-Board Strategies: How to Survive
and Win* (co-author)

*Talent Wins: The New Playbook for
Putting People First* (co-author)

*The High Potential Leader: How to
Grow Fast, Take on New Responsibility,
and Make an Impact*

*The Talent Masters: Why Smart Leaders
Put People Before Numbers*
(co-author)

*The Leadership Pipeline: How to
Build the Leadership Powered
Company* (co-author)

RETHINKING
COMPETITIVE
ADVANTAGE

RETHINKING
COMPETITIVE
ADVANTAGE

NEW RULES FOR THE DIGITAL AGE

RAM CHARAN

and Geri Willigan

CURRENCY

NEW YORK

Published in the United States by Currency, an imprint of Random
House, a division of Penguin Random House LLC, New York.

CURRENCY and its colophon are trademarks of
Penguin Random House LLC.

LIBRARY OF CONGRESS CATALOGING-IN-PUBLICATION DATA
Names: Charan, Ram, author. | Willigan, Geri, author.
Title: Rethinking competitive advantage / Ram Charan, Geri Willigan.
Description: First Edition. | New York : Currency, 2020. | Includes index.
Identifiers: LCCN 2020019338 (print) | LCCN 2020019339 (ebook) |
ISBN 9780525575603 (hardcover) | ISBN 9780525575610 (ebook)
Subjects: LCSH: Competition. | Consumer satisfaction. |
Leadership. | Organizational change.
Classification: LCC HD41 .C473 2020 (print) |
LCC HD41 (ebook) | DDC 658.4/062—dc23
LC record available at https://lccn.loc.gov/2020019338
LC ebook record available at https://lccn.loc.gov/2020019339

Printed in the United States of America on acid-free paper

crownpublishing.com

2 4 6 8 9 7 5 3 1

FIRST EDITION

Book design by Dana Leigh Blanchette

Dedicated to the hearts and souls of the joint family
of twelve siblings and cousins living under one roof
for fifty years, whose personal sacrifices made my
formal education possible.

CONTENTS

═══════════

INTRODUCTION: **WHY I WROTE THIS BOOK AND**   xiii
         HOW IT WILL HELP YOU

CHAPTER 1: **WHY THE DIGITAL GIANTS**   3
         ARE WINNING

CHAPTER 2: **NEW WORLD, NEW RULES**   19

CHAPTER 3: **MARKET SPACES OF 10X, 100X, 1000X**   31

CHAPTER 4: **DIGITAL PLATFORMS AT**   54
         THE CENTER OF THE BUSINESS

CHAPTER 5: **VALUE-CREATING ECOSYSTEMS**   83

CHAPTER 6: **MONEYMAKING FOR DIGITALS**   108

CHAPTER 7: **TEAMS INSTEAD OF ORGANIZATIONAL**   129
         LAYERS

CHAPTER 8: **LEADERS WHO CREATE WHAT'S NEXT**   159

CHAPTER 9: **RETHINKING COMPETITIVE ADVANTAGE**   175
          IN THE REAL WORLD

ACKNOWLEDGMENTS   181

APPENDIX: **ARE YOU READY TO BUILD COMPETITIVE**   185
          ADVANTAGE IN THE DIGITAL AGE?

NOTES   189

INDEX   193

THE NEW RULES OF COMPETITION

1. A personalized consumer experience is key to exponential growth.

2. Algorithms and data are essential weapons.

3. A company does not compete. Its ecosystem does.

4. Moneymaking is geared for huge cash generation, not earnings per share, and the new law of *increasing* returns. Funders understand the difference.

5. People, culture, and work design form a "social engine" that drives innovation and execution personalized for each customer.

6. Leaders continuously learn, imagine, and break through obstacles to create the change that other companies must contend with.

INTRODUCTION

WHY I WROTE THIS BOOK AND
HOW IT WILL HELP YOU

In my work with top leaders of digital and traditional companies around the globe, I kept hearing the same questions. Why have the dozen or so digital giants—these include Amazon, Facebook, Google, and Alibaba—grown so big so quickly? Will they continue to dominate? Do other companies even stand a chance to compete against them?

The digital giants have forever changed our experiences as consumers and employees. Lower prices, greater convenience, instant access to relevant information—all these things are now common expectations among consumers and even among businesses that buy from other businesses. And all are driven by digital technology, specifically the use of algorithms.

Algorithms—the mathematical rules by which data is processed—had existed for hundreds of years. When computers made it possible to process them very quickly and at low cost, people like Jeff Bezos of Amazon, Mark Zuckerberg of Facebook, and Larry Page and Sergey Brin of Google leapt at the chance to use them to solve a broad spectrum of problems. Unconstrained by management orthodoxy, these leaders let their imaginations soar. Some of the problems they tackled were small, as in Bezos's initial desire to offer readers a vast selection of books at a low price; his ambition expanded from there. Others were big, as in Google's aim to "organize the world's information."

The impact of these exceptional leaders and organizations is obvious, but the why and how of their success are not. So I set out to study exactly why and how the digital giants turned the competitive order on its head.

My research over the past five years made one fact crystal clear: Creating competitive advantage is different in the digital age. Until recently the greatest competitive advantage went to companies that controlled distribution channels, had hard assets on the largest scale, or had established brands or patents. Today those advantages no longer ensure that a company will outcompete others.

In the digital age, competitive advantage is the ability to win the ultimate prize—the consumer's preference—*repeatedly*, through continuous innovation on behalf of the consumer, and to create immense value for shareholders at the same time.

Competitive advantage comes as much from what a company *does* as from what a company *has:* how it perceives the consumer experience, selects leaders, organizes work, and makes money as well as its ecosystem and access to data and funding. The sources of competitive advantage, once developed, can be hard for traditional companies to match, because they are ingrained (a mindset for exponential growth and an action-oriented culture). They are cumulative (more data leads to better consumer insights; larger scale generates more cash). And they are systemic (better predictions lead to more customer satisfaction and lower costs, which in turn increase revenues and cash gross margin, which provides the cash to innovate and serve the consumer better).

This book has two main purposes: to fully explain the sources of a digital giant's formidable competitive advantage, and to help other companies see a path to building theirs. From my observation of digital companies, I have identified a new set of rules for creating competitive advantage. These new rules explain what *any company*—whether it is a digital giant or a traditional company—must do to prosper in this digital age. For legacy companies that are becoming digital, this book will fill in the pieces that leaders often miss when they focus on technology alone. For example, it might encourage them to be bolder in redesigning how work gets done as they build their digital capability (see chapter 7 on how Fidelity Personal Investing did just that).

For traditional companies that have not yet begun to move, this book is a call to action. By explaining how digital companies compound their competitive advantages, it shows how quickly traditional advantages can erode and how inadequate existing mindsets and tools have become. The gap between the digitals and nondigitals widened during the coronavirus outbreak, when digital companies were able to adjust quickly to the abrupt changes in consumer behavior, supply chains, and work life, and their competitive advantage in moneymaking gave them more cash to sustain the business.

In April 2020, in the midst of the pandemic, Netflix CEO Reed Hastings wrote a letter to shareholders posted to Netflix's website for investors that reassuringly reminded them that "Netflix's culture is designed to empower decision making at all levels of the company." He went on to say that within two weeks of the shelter-in-place orders going into effect in Los Angeles, most of their animation production team was back up and running, working from home. On the postproduction side, they were able to get 200+ projects going remotely. And most of their series writers' rooms were operating virtually.

The coronavirus shock was extreme. But even in a normal period, the burning question is: Against today's digital behemoths, do others stand a chance? Unequivocally, yes. Traditional companies across the board are in the early stages of becoming digital. The ones that rethink their competitive advantage sooner will quickly overtake their peers and, yes, they can challenge born-digital players. Amazon boomed during the coronavirus pandemic. So did Walmart, because it was further along in digitizing its business than many legacy retailers.

No competitive advantage is ironclad. It must be earned on a daily basis. Amazon still dominates e-commerce, but Walmart is on the rise. For years Netflix was virtually alone in the video streaming market space, but now digital giants Amazon and Apple have ramped up their presence, along with traditional players Disney, NBC, and WarnerMedia.

Netflix subscribers surged to 182 million in the first three months of 2020 when everyone was stuck at home, but by late April 2020, Disney+ had amassed a respectable 50 million subscribers, NBCUniversal launched that month with 15 million, and AT&T's awaited launch of HBO Max was imminent.

The means for gaining competitive advantage are increasingly available. Algorithms and expertise can be acquired at relatively low cost. And funding continues to flow to companies that adopt metrics and models that reflect the new fundamentals of moneymaking.

Knowing the new rules of competition will raise your perspective and help you set the course in the complex and fast-changing landscape.

Chapter 1 explains the underlying forces that have turned a handful of start-ups into trillion-dollar-market-value giants in fewer than twenty-five years. My point is to show you exactly why they have changed the competitive landscape, and what it means for your future. Chapter 2 describes some conventional business practices that no longer work and some common beliefs that must be dispelled.

Chapters 3 through 8 explain each of the new rules for creating competitive advantage and use real-company examples to show how to put them to work Monday morning. Chapter 9 will give you encouragement to act by showing how quickly some legacy companies have moved.

It has been my mission in life to provide insights and knowledge that are useful to practitioners. I hope this book succeeds in that mission.

RETHINKING
COMPETITIVE
ADVANTAGE

CHAPTER 1

═══════

WHY THE DIGITAL GIANTS
ARE WINNING

In February 2019, as Hollywood's elite convened for the 91st Academy Awards ceremony, Netflix found itself in a war of words with famed director Steven Spielberg. *Green Book,* the movie Spielberg had backed, won the Oscar for Best Picture. But Spielberg made it clear that he didn't think *Roma,* another strong contender that had been produced by Netflix, should have been in the running for an Oscar at all.

Spielberg's argument against *Roma* was that it was streamed by Netflix directly to consumers after an exclusive run of just three weeks in movie theaters. Traditional films are shown in theaters for months at a time. Shortcutting a theatrical release, Spielberg argued, deprives moviegoers of an immersive big-screen experience and puts the entire theater system at risk.

As the Academy's board of governors prepared to debate the issue, one governor remarked: "The rules were put into effect when no one could conceive of this present or this future."

Actually, Netflix CEO and cofounder Reed Hastings conceived of this future nearly two decades ago, before broadband was widely used. Then Hastings did what leaders of every successful digital company do. He exploited new technology to create the future he imagined much faster than other people thought possible.

Imagining new market spaces and revenue pools that can scale up at unprecedented speed is just one way that born-digital companies—those that were digital from the start—have gained a huge competitive edge in recent years. Thinking differently about how to make money and fund growth is a second way. And using algorithmic technology to reorganize work and enhance decision-making is yet a third.

In today's competitive age, traditional companies need to know what they're up against and learn from the born-digital players how to build competitive advantage.

The New Nature of Competition

Back in 2000, even as Netflix built its competitive advantage by sending out DVDs by mail as opposed to having consumers visit retail video stories like Blockbuster, its leaders knew that broadband technology would someday be fast enough, cheap enough, and good enough for consumers to watch movies sent or streamed to their devices directly, anywhere at any time. The technology still wasn't advanced enough in 2005 when Hastings told *Inc.* magazine's Patrick J. Sauer: "We want to be ready when video-on-demand happens."

In 2007, the time had come. About half of U.S. residences had access to broadband, and Netflix was ready to begin streaming movies into the homes of its customers. YouTube was experiencing rapid growth, and Hulu, owned in partnership between NBC and Comcast, sprang up around the same time. Netflix flourished because of a powerful combination of elements.

For one thing, Netflix charged a monthly subscription fee that gave consumers access to unlimited videos—a novelty at a time when most people rented one or a few DVDs or VHS tapes at a time. To be sure that consumers would not run out of new things to watch, Netflix licensed content from traditional media companies. Subscribers could watch popular new film releases without leaving home and for the first time could binge-watch their favorite old TV shows.

None of that would have been possible without a technology platform that could deliver a smooth viewing experience. But Netflix's digital platform didn't just transmit signals through broadband connections—it also gathered data about its customers' viewing habits along the way. Algorithms got increasingly better at analyzing that data to help subscribers find content they liked amid a widening array of options.

Building its digital platform, securing broadband spectrum, paying licensing fees, and hiring technology experts to write and refine the algorithms all contributed to Netflix's skyrocketing revenue and subscriber growth. These efforts also consumed cash, more than Netflix was generating in its quest for ultra-fast scaling and building its streaming capability.

It famously tried to sell itself to Blockbuster early on, but Blockbuster turned it down. Instead, Netflix managed to find shareholders and lenders who believed in its future and knew the reasons for Netflix's cash drain. Earnings per share, or EPS, could wait. The waiting was extended as Netflix ventured into creating its own content, beginning with the series *House of Cards,* which went into development in 2009 and was released four years later.

It was a full decade later, in early 2019, before some of the largest media companies like WarnerMedia, Disney, and Apple mounted a serious challenge to Netflix's dominance in streaming. And Amazon, another major player that had entered the space, shored up its presence. In the first quarter of 2019, a series of competitive actions and reactions kicked into gear.

In February 2019, the U.S. Justice Department cleared the merger of Time Warner and AT&T, which aimed to help the entities compete against digital players that both created and distributed content, and senior management immediately began to reassemble the pieces. The former head of NBC Entertainment, Robert Greenblatt, was put in charge of WarnerMedia, a new combination of HBO and parts of Turner Broadcasting, and tasked with designing a new streaming service.

A month later, on March 20, 2019, Disney closed on its $71.3 billion deal to buy a big chunk of Twentieth Century Fox, which included the film and TV studios and a 30 percent stake in Hulu. Disney already owned 30 percent of Hulu, so it now had a majority stake. Meanwhile, Disney had been winding down its licensing arrangements with Netflix and hyping its imminent release of Disney+, a streaming service separate from Hulu.

Five days later Apple announced it would launch a TV app in the fall that would distribute content from HBO, Showtime, and other sources for a monthly fee. Steven Spielberg himself stood on the stage when Apple CEO Tim Cook explained that the service would include original content Apple was creating.

That quarter Amazon secured rights to a TV series based on *Lord of the Rings,* with a whopping budget of $1 billion, according to some reports. The news prompted media analyst Rich Greenfield to comment: "There is an all-out war for the control of your media life. I think the reality is these big tech platforms, who have valuations and market caps and cash piles that are massive relative to traditional media, they are just getting started."

The series of announcements so closely timed set Twitter ablaze. How many subscription services would people pay for? Would bureaucracy at WarnerMedia snuff out the creativity of HBO? Would Disney's new business model mean a price cut for movie streaming? What would be bundled and what wouldn't? And will Netflix, a current favorite with consumers, continue to flourish and lead the way?

Competitive Action and Reaction

Video streaming is just one example of a digital economy where competition is intensifying. Many so-called legacy companies are caught up in a battle with digital competitors, and so far, the born-digital companies have been eating their lunch. Walmart (and every other physical retail store, from Macy's to Best Buy) is in a constant duel with Amazon, and banks and credit card companies are squaring off against PayPal and Apple Pay.

Meanwhile the digital giants are battling each other for market share and dominance: Amazon's AWS (Amazon Web Services) versus Microsoft's Azure cloud services. Consumer goods companies, retailers, and manufacturers have hundreds of e-commerce start-ups nibbling at the edges of their market share with niche products sold directly to consumers online. Think of P&G's Gillette razors sold in stores versus the online subscription-based Dollar Shave Club that sells direct to consumers.

The common thread in these erupting battles is digitization. It has upended the very nature of competition today, and made twentieth-century ways of thinking about competitive advantage obsolete.

The old adage "stick to your knitting," for example, a colloquial version of "build on your core competence," tends to narrow a company's imagination. Yet a bold imagination is a requirement for leaders today. Netflix, Amazon, Facebook, and Google would not be what they are if their

CEOs and executive teams had not imagined a future that did not yet exist.

A clear view of the competitive landscape suggests that some of the early generalizations about "first mover advantage" and "winner takes all" are not holding up, especially as digital giants challenge each other.

First movers may be able to scale up fast, but others are certain to enter whatever large market spaces they create. For that reason, winners really don't take it all, at least not forever. And if new competitors don't enter the fray quickly enough, antitrust government regulators may step in.

As early and dominant as Amazon has been in e-commerce, it is hardly alone. Alibaba, Tencent, and JD.com are fierce global competitors, and traditional retailer Walmart is barreling into the online space in a bigger way since its acquisition of Jet.com and its majority stake in Flipkart, India's largest e-commerce player. It has been gaining traction by linking its online sales with physical stores. In Brazil, B2W has held Amazon, a relative newcomer, at bay.

The outcome of these competitive battles is uncertain. But some fundamental differences in how digital companies compete have become clear.

When one dissects the Netflixes, Amazons, Googles, and Alibabas of the world, we see that they have certain elements in common:

- *They imagine a 100x market space that doesn't yet exist.* They imagine an end-to-end experience in a person's life—as the individual travels, eats, shops for goods, or seeks medical care or entertainment—that could be greatly improved, and if it were, that a vast number of people would want. They think about how technology could be used to make the seemingly impossible happen. They focus on the end user even if intermediaries lie between them and the consumer. They know that if their offering is right for the end user, they can scale up very quickly, because word spreads almost instantaneously. Netflix believed that a huge number of people would prefer to discover and enjoy videos at their convenience in their homes instead of going to a movie theater and putting up with overpriced snacks and disturbing neighbors, or watching TV at prescribed times set by the entertainment companies or networks. In the age of $50 cellphones and ultra-low-cost Internet connections, as in India, the potential market explodes.

- *They have a digital platform at their core.* A digital platform is an expertly stitched together mix of algorithms that store and analyze data for a variety of purposes. It allows for fast experimentation and fast adjustment of prices, and makes it possible to reach a huge population globally at minimal incremental cost. Netflix can easily stream its repertoire across geographic borders. Algorithms in the categories of artificial intelligence and machine learning can correct themselves as they learn more about customers' behavior and preferences, improving personalization and thereby increasing customer loyalty.

- **They have an ecosystem that accelerates their growth.** Ecosystem partners take many forms, such as third-party sellers on Amazon's website, Uber's independent drivers, or Apple's app developers. They allow the company to expand capacity quickly, often with no capital investment on its part. They allow cross-selling to extend innovations to a broader audience. They can also enable a new moneymaking model or supply a capability that is missing. Most ecosystems share data, contributing to the ability to scale up fast. Netflix would not exist without the content it licensed from its ecosystem, such as the TV series *Friends* from WarnerMedia and *The Office* from NBCUniversal. Companies don't compete against each other—their ecosystems do.

- **Their moneymaking is tied to cash and exponential growth.** Digital businesses know that after a period of intense cash consumption, if the offering is successful, returns will turn sharply upward as the incremental cost of the next unit sold or subscriber added drops. They focus more on cash than on accounting measures. Funders who recognize the law of *increasing returns* are willing to ease the liquidity issues in the early going to reap exponential rewards later.*

* W. Brian Arthur, external faculty member at Santa Fe Institute, IBM faculty fellow, and visiting researcher in Intelligent Systems Lab at PARC, described the phenomenon of increasing returns in the early 1990s. See *Increasing Returns and Path Dependence in the Economy* (Ann Arbor: University of Michigan Press, 1994).

- *Decision-making is designed for innovation and speed.* The downside of growth and a principal reason traditional companies experience *diminishing returns* is the increased complexity and bureaucracy that come with growth. But increased bureaucracy is not a given for companies that have a digital platform at their center. Teams close to the action can make decisions and take action without layers of oversight because they can easily access real-time information. They can move very fast. Accountability is built in because the digital platform makes a team's progress visible to anyone in the company who needs to know. Overhead is kept to a minimum even as the company expands rapidly; Amazon's general and administrative costs are just 1.5 percent of revenues. Recruiting people who are self-motivated and can thrive in a team-based environment makes the company innovative and agile.

- *Their leaders drive learning, reinvention, and execution.* Digital leaders have a different set of skills and competencies than traditional managers. They have a working knowledge of technology, an expansive imagination, and an ability to link their big-picture thinking with ground-level execution. Their use of data takes execution to a whole new level. And their constant communication with their teams, along with their decisiveness in shifting resources, makes the organization agile. The fluidity of their thinking drives continuous change and growth. They create the change that leaders of many other companies struggle to contend with.

So today's digital giants and upstarts focus intensely on the experience of an individual consumer and open big new market spaces. They scale up fast, aggregate data, and draw relevant partners into their ecosystem. Their business models focus on cash gross margin (a new metric explained in chapter 6), cash generation, and exponential growth. They get hefty amounts of cash to fund their growth from VCs and investors who understand the new patterns of money-making. And their highly committed leaders and employees work with purpose and focus relentlessly on what's next, driving speed, continuous innovation, and disciplined execution.

These elements of the digital giants are especially powerful in combination.

Let's look again at Netflix.

At most companies, CEOs are reminded quarterly, if not daily, that earnings per share is sacrosanct. If earnings slip for more than a few quarters, their leadership is questioned.

Reed Hastings, on the other hand, doesn't live and breathe EPS—and that was especially so when he was growing Netflix into a worldwide brand. While he was waiting for broadband to take hold, he invested heavily in the technology for streaming. The company also invested heavily in getting the best (and most highly paid) technology people and software engineers available. Hastings, a software engineer himself, knew that the ability to keep improving Netflix's algorithms was critical: first, to ensure that videos would be transmitted from whichever location would provide the best viewing experience; and second, to help subscribers find the content they wanted amid an ever-expanding range of options.

Those viewing options consisted of movies and TV shows other companies created and Netflix licensed. The licensing fees the traditional players collected looked good on their income statements. They boosted revenues and earnings for content they had already created.

But what Netflix got from those licensing deals in the early years was arguably more valuable: a very bright future. The expanding catalog kept existing subscribers interested and induced new ones to sign up. Netflix's growth curve tipped upward, increasing its cash flow.

Hastings anticipated that some ecosystem partners, over time, would let their licensing agreements expire and enter the streaming market themselves somewhere along the line. To ensure that the catalog continued to expand, in 2009 the company began to channel money to original content. The company analyzed its trove of data on people's viewing preferences to decide what kind of story to produce and which actors to sign.

Netflix experimented with that data-driven approach to create its first original series, *House of Cards*. Released in 2013, the series was a huge success with both subscribers and critics, drawing in hordes of new subscribers and making it easier to attract top creative talent to future projects.

Since then, Netflix has continued to refine its algorithms and has dramatically increased its R&D spend to create a wide range of original movies and series. It spent $15 billion on original content in 2019.

Throughout Netflix's evolution, Hastings has been focused on giving consumers an exceptional viewing experience, ensuring they could find the content they liked, and leveraging what technology could do at a given point in time. As long as consumers were getting an exceptional viewing experience at great value, the thinking goes, they would continue to subscribe, providing a steady flow of cash. Increasing the subscriber base would continue to build credibility with investors and lenders and keep the investment funds flowing.

As Netflix grew, its bureaucracy did not. The company has been able to maintain a lean reporting hierarchy because of how it screens new hires for competence and ability to work in autonomous teams, and how it uses digital technology to make performance and accountability transparent.

None of this means that legacy companies can't shape an equally brilliant future (chapters 4 and 7 show how B2W and Fidelity did). But they will have to learn from the digital juggernauts and make some changes.

On the surface, entertainment giants like Netflix, Amazon, Disney, WarnerMedia, and Apple seem well matched. All have tremendous resources. WarnerMedia and Disney, with their extensive libraries of movies and TV content, have no real barriers to entering the streaming market space, just as Netflix, Amazon, and Apple have no real barriers to creating their own original content.

[Handwritten note: Do we really understand consumer preference?]

T… experience of … ata, along with … xperience. How … database and … azon have, to b… ences?

… at deal of mo… What is the bas… ions affect ma… attract talent

… in placing bet… ck in with generous compensation. Contracts with the top actors, writers, and directors can be key to providing better value to subscribers.

Movie studios have extensive expertise in determining when to launch a movie, in how many theaters, on which weekend, and how to advertise them. (The ad spend sometimes eclipses the cost of making the movie.) They may later get residuals for showing movies on TV or someone else's streaming service. How would all of that be affected by doing more streaming? Would other revenue streams dry up? How quickly?

Disney had already seen its revenues begin to decline, while Fox basically opted out of the new game by selling off its moviemaking assets.

The moneymaking model for streaming is entirely different. Digital distribution follows the law of *increasing returns*. Global expansion is easier, and the cost of serving each new viewer is lower than the one before. After the initial spend for content and technology, incremental costs steadily drop. Some VCs and investment firms compete to support companies whose moneymaking models are based on this principle. How might new business models blend digital and theatrical releases?

Any successful organization has to accept that consumers' tastes and expectations will continue to change, as will the technology underpinning their moneymaking model. Companies have to constantly revisit the consumer's end-to-end experience with an eye toward improving it or totally redesigning it.

Dissatisfaction with the status quo and a search for what's next is a universal human endeavor. It does not reside in one person, department, or organizational layer. The flow of ideas cannot be blocked by bureaucratic layers. Do the people at traditional companies welcome change? What happens to the good ideas that emerge? How quickly do they get converted into action?

Will the leaders of traditional players be able to reshape their organizations' practices and mindsets fast enough to stem the declines in revenues and overtake players that continue to build scale?

Established companies have enviable resources, brands, customer bases, talent pools, and data that digital start-ups envy. But going forward, that will not be enough. Sooner or later every company will be pitted against a digital competitor who is playing by different rules. To successfully compete, you have to know what they are and follow them. The next chapter explains them.

CHAPTER 2

NEW WORLD, NEW RULES

Netflix exponentially expanded and redefined the entertainment space from movies shown in theaters and linear TV to streaming of content on multiple devices, anytime, anyplace, even globally. Amazon, Airbnb, Uber, Lyft, and other digital companies also redefined their market spaces. Traditional companies are now rethinking their own use of digital technology and preparing to play a different game. Some are hiring chief digital officers, beefing up their data analytics departments, and enlisting consulting firms to guide them through a digital transformation. Others are renting space in a technology hot spot to build their own digital start-up. They are having to figure out how to take resources from the core business, which may be facing intensifying competition, to build a future that is uncertain.

Their challenge is to build a digital core soon enough to survive the inevitable decline in their existing business. As I work with CEOs and C-suite leaders daily, I hear their deep concern about their company's dwindling growth rates.

Single-digit revenue growth is the norm, and, for some, revenues and profits are actually declining and investors are selling out. Their revenue curve looks like this:

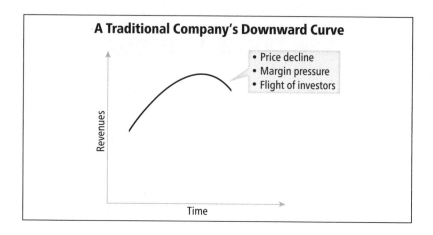

A Traditional Company's Downward Curve

- Price decline
- Margin pressure
- Flight of investors

Revenues

Time

The damage to these once-thriving businesses comes from two directions: first, from digital players that have entered their space with a superior customer offering and moneymaking model, and second, from traditional competitors who cut prices in their own desperation to survive, an approach that can destroy the profitability of an entire industry. Retail is a case in point. Already beaten up competitively, JCPenney, Neiman Marcus, and J. Crew had to file for bankruptcy when Covid-19 hit.

Any company seeking a way forward must start by understanding the new rules of competition. Let's review the rules that successful digital companies seem to follow from the front of the book.

THE NEW RULES OF COMPETITION

1. A personalized consumer experience is key to exponential growth.

2. Algorithms and data are essential weapons.

3. A company does not compete. Its ecosystem does.

4. Moneymaking is geared for huge cash generation, not earnings per share, and the new law of *increasing* returns. Funders understand the difference.

5. People, culture, and work design form a "social engine" that drives innovation and execution personalized for each customer.

6. Leaders continuously learn, imagine, and break through obstacles to create the change that other companies must contend with.

Today's digital giants discovered these new rules by accident. Most of the founders spent little if any time in conventional companies or attending business schools. Mark Zuckerberg dropped out of college, as did Steve Jobs and Bill Gates before him. They simply saw how technology could transform people's lives and found novel ways to get the resources and talent they needed to deliver what they imagined.

When a belief or a practice worked, they stuck with it and built on it, and they picked up good ideas from other companies, including each other. They may have known only intuitively at the start how powerful these rules would prove to be, especially in combination.

What Is Different and What Is Not

The drive to dominate in business has never changed. The digital giants are no less determined to expand and set the pace for others than any corporation has been.

The fundamental components of moneymaking also are the same. Revenue, gross margin, net profit, cash flow, and capital investment are universal concepts that apply to every type of business in every country throughout the world. They will never change, although the relationships among them are now different, as I'll explain in chapter 6.

Some conventional competitive advantages persist, such as brand, reputation, patents, and proprietary technologies. And for capital-intensive businesses like steel and car

manufacturing, <u>scale still matte</u>rs. But many of the traditional barriers to entry no longer hold. Scale of distribution, for example, is not a barrier when companies sell
direct to the consumer. Procter & Gamble, Kimberly-Clark,
and Unilever have well-developed distribution chains and
long-standing deep relationships with the retail chains that
give their consumer products shelf space, but Amazon by-
passes that barrier by delivering products directly to a customer's door.

By far the biggest difference in creating competitive advantage before and after the arrival of the digital age is the
speed of competitive action and reaction. All companies
now operate in an extremely fast lane that presents twists
and turns without notice.

That means no matter how well a company is doing, the
business can fall behind quickly when a new competitor
suddenly cuts in. Amazon's Jeff Bezos, who has upped the
frequency and speed of change for so many other companies, understands that success is never permanent. His famous "Day 1" mantra (also the name of the building that
houses his office) reflects a daily fight against complacency.
As he wrote in his first annual report in 1997, "Day 2 is
stasis. Followed by irrelevance. Followed by excruciating,
painful decline. Followed by death. And *that* is why it is *always* Day 1."

Every sharp move triggers decisive responses from the
leading players, so the competitive order is in constant flux.
GM, Ford, and Chrysler enjoyed their dominant position in
car manufacturing for decades before the underdog Japa-

nese automakers outdid the Americans with new management systems and manufacturing techniques. In the digital age, no company will go unchallenged for that long.

Today when somebody launches a new idea in the marketplace—think Uber or Spotify or Instagram—that business can mature very fast. Distribution systems that required enormous financial resources to build can be circumvented. Consumers, even those in far-flung places, can learn about new offerings almost instantly, thanks to social media. So you have to earn your place—continuously. Competitive advantage will be short-lived unless you continuously innovate for the customer, and search for and execute on new avenues of revenue growth.

The Roadblocks to Moving Forward

In the rest of the book I will explain what you need to know in order to understand and adopt the new rules of competition. At the same time, you have to let go of assumptions and beliefs that held true in the past and have been drilled into you for most of your career. They are often impediments now, limiting your perspective and imagination. Here are some common ones:

An overreliance on outdated theories. The guiding lights that a generation of business leaders relied on to grow and compete were created decades ago. The economy has changed since Michael Porter redefined strategic planning with his classic books, *Competitive Strategy* and *Competitive Advantage,* in the 1980s, and since the late C. K. Prahalad and Gary Hamel taught us about strategic intent and core competence in the following decade. Concepts from thought leaders in an earlier age at Bain & Company, McKinsey & Company, and Boston Consulting Group (BCG) have been tremendously helpful to thousands of business leaders worldwide and are mainstays of MBA programs. Yet they fall short when it comes to giving companies a competitive edge in today's digital economy.

Porter's five forces analysis is focused mainly on gaining market share by managing entry and exit barriers and deploying one of two generic strategies: lower cost or differentiation. The model advocates that firms build sustainable competitive advantages through patents, brand recognition, distribution, or scale, which require enormous capital investment. But many of those barriers have not been able to fend off Amazon, Alibaba, and other e-commerce companies.

Competitive analysis has been based on a set of known players in a single, clearly delineated industry. Since then, Uber, Lyft, and other ride-share companies have intruded into the auto industry and caused us to define a new "mobility" market space. Suddenly Uber is stealing away customers who might have bought Ford or GM products. Similarly, the boundaries of the hotel industry have blurred now that travelers can access unused space in people's homes or book travel "experiences" that include unconventional lodging, such as treehouses and boats, and activities like wine tasting and music via Airbnb.

Change used to occur incrementally and more slowly; companies spent weeks and months analyzing the competitive landscape and forging a rock-solid strategy, one they intended to endure for years. Today transformational change is the norm. Every company has to be able to perceive what will make their best-laid plans obsolete tomorrow and change direction quickly.

Trying to build on your core competence can be a liability in the digital age. Why? Because it tends to promote an inside-out perspective and narrow a leader's peripheral vision and constrain imagination. It tends to lead to incremental moves into adjacent segments (Nike going into athletic apparel, or Hertz expanding into truck rentals) or to look for new uses for existing brands (WD-40, developed for rust prevention, now sold as a general-purpose product useful for dozens of applications from waterproofing gloves to cleaning golf clubs), rather than creating a new market space.

Core competencies have a shelf life. They become obsolete, and new ones have to be built. Today, because of the availability of information, the consumer rules the day, yet rarely do I see a company describe a core competence in understanding the end-to-end consumer experience. Traditional retailers woke up late to the reality of needing to build their competence in e-commerce. Walmart, under the leadership of CEO Doug McMillon, bought Jet.com to build its online capability and is experimenting with how to combine online sales with sales in brick-and-mortar stores.

Companies that stick too long with a narrow view of their core competence and fail to build newly required capabilities will suffer badly. Netflix and Hulu built streaming capability early. Disney, Apple, Amazon, and WarnerMedia did so many years later. Fox dragged its feet in building competence in streaming but sold its movie assets to Disney soon enough to avoid serious financial damage.

Even portfolio or capital allocation models, such as BCG's famous matrix that sorts businesses into one of four quadrants (cash cows, stars, dogs, and question marks) based on market share and growth rate, fall short by assuming that current realities—and therefore what the business should focus on—are largely static.

*A **dominant psychology of incrementalism and short-term thinking.*** Leaders who have built their careers in companies that are largely focused on earnings per share and market share are 100 percent focused on one year out, even if they also do three-year projections. This is partly driven by their compensation incentives. When I go to see CEOs and ask them what is happening, it's uncanny how similar they sound. They say something like "Our quarter is in good shape," or "We beat P&G last quarter." Their orientation is to get those near-term metrics up, if only by a little bit.

Compare that to Netflix, where CEO Reed Hastings focuses on how many subscribers are on the platform and what their level of engagement is. He can monitor those metrics on a daily basis and make adjustments. But he is also oriented toward making decisions for the longer term. Netflix anticipated the possibility of losing access to other companies' film and television rights and moved preemptively to start creating its own content.

*A **blind spot when it comes to customers.*** As a member of seven different corporate boards, I have reviewed approx-

imately twenty strategic business plans from major corporations a year for the past twenty-five years. They are usually
presented in a series of a hundred or more PowerPoint slides
at a two-day retreat with the corporate board at some ritzy
venue. The presentations are heavy with assumptions about
the future, past historical data, and accomplishments, and
include so-called SWOT analysis (strengths, weaknesses, opportunities, and threats). They typically show a hockey-stick
graph of sharply rising numbers after a decline in next year's
performance. Many are prepared with the help of a high-
caliber consulting firm.

Guess what they don't include, ever. They never show
the shelf life of their competitive advantage. They omit a
clear description of why the consumer prefers them. They
reflect no deep understanding of the end-to-end customer
experience, which includes every interaction with the company from first exposure to the product or service to usage
and repairs or service later. Finally, and most important,
they ignore future competitors that may come into their
space and how the competitive actions and reactions might
play out.

When fierce competitors Coca-Cola and Pepsi diligently
tracked customers' preferences in the 1980s, the focus was
more quantitative than qualitative. But numbers alone do
not give decision makers the tools they need to evaluate the
leading indicators and anticipate shifts in consumer behavior that will be reflected in the numbers later. Most leaders
who have risen through the ranks in traditional companies
are stuck in the narrow numbers game.

Acceptance of existing boundaries. Until recently, organizing companies into industries, and later industry sectors, served a purpose. Besides defining the playing field for companies, it also helped investors and analysts make meaningful comparisons. Usually those definitions—aerospace, defense, or automotive—were based on physical descriptions of the products companies made. Analysts sometimes griped about the difficulty of tracking companies, such as GE, that competed in multiple industries, but they found ways to simulate a peer group.

Digital giants pay no attention to what industry they should or should not be in. They focus relentlessly on the consumer and are determined to provide a new consumer experience where they see an opening. They think in terms of a more complete end-to-end experience, which generally touches on multiple traditional industries. While Netflix streams entertainment, it also has the capability to disseminate educational products. Amazon began in retail but is also a major player in logistics, cloud computing, and advertising.

While traditional competitors feel the need to go it alone, the digital giants are not confined by their own four walls. If they do not have the capability to deliver what the customer needs, they seek ways to get it from outside players. They think in terms of open systems and ecosystems. When Tencent wanted to extend its WeChat social media service to Chinese tourists visiting Europe, it partnered with KPN, the Dutch telecom and IT giant, which created a SIM card and lined up telecom service in less than three months.

The same difference in mental boundaries applies to

funding. Traditional companies are more apt to assume that investors and lenders will react as they always have—with skepticism—if they were to pursue an ambitious and costly growth plan. Having a track record of delivering on promises clearly helps, but the digital giants do not rein in their ambition for fear that they cannot fund it.

Belief in mass markets and segmentation. Our major strides in the standard of living over the last century were the result of the mass production of goods, which made them affordable for a large portion of the population. Mass production was a huge generational shift from the cottage-industry era that preceded it. Through much of the twentieth century, mass production and mass markets evolved into market segments; for example, Ford's one-size-fits-all Model T led to GM's range of models, which every automaker has offered ever since.

The use of algorithms to personalize a customer experience, in most instances also at lower cost, is changing expectations yet again. The reality that algorithms make it possible to deliver a personalized experience at low cost must sink in and get factored into the design and/or delivery of every product and service. Using the economics of mass production to gain share of a mass market is no longer a reliable path to competitive advantage. Against a digital competitor, even aiming to serve a market segment might not be good enough. Leaders should strive for personalization at every touch point in the customer journey. As you will see in the next chapter, an earnest search will reveal opportunities to create a huge new market space.

CHAPTER 3

MARKET SPACES OF 10X, 100X, 1000X

Rule #1: A personalized consumer experience is key to exponential growth.

Opportunities in the digital age can be vastly bigger than at any previous time in business history. Leaders of digital businesses recognize this potential. It's part of their DNA to seek opportunities that they can scale up quickly. They think in terms of markets that can grow 10 times, 100 times, or even 1000 times bigger than the current market space.

In the 1970s, when corporations' information processing was powered by large mainframe computers that sold for millions of dollars, Bill Gates imagined a world in which there was a computer on every desk and in every home. It would be, he believed, an enormous market. Personal computers, or PCs, did not exist, but technology had begun to move in that direction, with greater computing power on smaller semiconductor chips manufactured at increasingly lower cost. So why wouldn't Gates's notion be credible as the industry continued to evolve? Of course it was, and today most of us have an affordable, easy-to-use computer in our pockets in the form of our cellphones.

Traditional retailers have long been limited by the geographic radius in which they operate. It takes a long time, relatively speaking, and a lot of capital to expand their reach. But the Internet obliterates those geographic boundaries. It puts virtually all of the world's 7.2 billion people within the reach of digital giants such as Amazon, Alibaba, JD.com, Tencent, Rakuten, B2W, and today, finally, Walmart. It took Walmart more than fifty years to reach a market value of $337 billion. Amazon has created almost three times that market value—some $940 billion as of the beginning of 2020—in fewer than twenty-five years. Its revenues went from zero to $280 billion in that time, growing 20 percent from 2018 to 2019 in that one year alone.

The leaders of today's digital giants bring unbounded imagination and big-picture thinking to the equation. But what also distinguishes their thinking is that they keep a laser focus on the individual consumer in everything they do. The consumer drives every decision that they make.

First, they dig deep for insights into the consumer's behavior. And using their basic understanding of algorithmic technology, they form an idea about how to transform some slice of the consumer's total life experience. They develop a concrete vision of the consumer experience they want to create and the specific reasons why the consumer will prefer it.

The foremost question for these digital leaders as they

make decisions about their company is: How will individual consumers benefit from this? They work relentlessly on behalf of the individual consumer and reshape the business landscape in whatever way makes sense to deliver the experience they imagine. When they get that vision right, word spreads fast (through the Internet), and the new market space expands quickly. Sometimes consumers change their behavior as a result, and their expectations change almost continuously.

Offering free two-day delivery in the United States for a fixed annual fee was a risky move for Amazon over a decade ago. But CEO Jeff Bezos started with the premise that customers would want it and relied on his company's enormous operational skills and its use of data and algorithms to illuminate how they could make it economically viable. Amazon figured out where to build new distribution centers and how to use technology to run them ultra-efficiently. It now has an unparalleled core competence in logistics. According to a former Amazon executive, delivery cost was ultimately reduced by a factor of 10.

New ideas for meeting consumer needs coupled with granularity and follow-through are far more potent than purely aspirational statements such as "We'll be bigger than competitor X" or "We aim to reach revenues of $200 billion."

Today, thanks to Amazon and others, everyone expects fast delivery and convenience. That includes companies that buy from other businesses. It's an expectation that is putting many traditional competitors on defense and forcing them to change. These players are at a disadvantage because they must compete in a fast-changing market space that someone else has defined. Whether Uber survives in the long term or not, it and other ride-sharing companies like Lyft and Didi Chuxing have catalyzed major automakers to adjust to the changing economics of their business. Carmakers are retreating from some geographies, radically shrinking the number of models they offer, and shifting their focus from manufacturing to mobility.

Walmart has sprung to life and is fighting back against Amazon. It has been building its e-commerce business and seeking ways to link it with their physical stores. In Brazil, traditional retailer Lojas Americanas created B2W, an e-commerce start-up that has stayed far ahead of Amazon and Walmart, which entered Latin America later. In India, where Amazon and Walmart compete against each other—Walmart via a majority stake it bought in Indian e-commerce giant Flipkart—the two digital giants are being challenged by an online start-up funded by Reliance Industries, India's second-largest company. Reliance is using the enormous amount of cash its refinery business generates to put JioMart on equal footing with the two e-commerce leaders. As of early 2020, all three businesses were losing money and consuming cash.

One of the greatest advantages leaders of born-digital companies have, I would argue, is their psychological freedom to imagine something that doesn't exist and how a consumer can benefit from it. Everything their companies do is anchored to the realities of the consumer experience and how to make a slice of their life experience better. The adjectives that come to mind are *cheaper, faster, more con-*

venient, and *hassle-free*. And they apply to banking, search, social media, shopping, entertainment, travel—you name the human endeavor.

These leaders do not seem to be constrained by the company's existing capabilities. Even when they have a well-developed core competence, they do not get stuck trying to leverage it. They are more concerned with what new experience customers will want. They don't accept the usual boundaries of industry, market space, or market segments. In fact, they often knit together activities from multiple industries to realize their vision (see chapter 5 for more on this).

The Great Mind Shift

Most companies reach the consumer through several links in the distribution chain. A company that manufactures refrigerators sells its products to retail outlets like Best Buy and P. C. Richard, where consumers shop for various makes and models. Manufacturers usually consider the retail outlet their customer.

Many corporations have been successful for decades by virtue of their strong relationships with the players that are next in the value chain. As long as a company understood what its immediate customers wanted and kept them happy, its business was secure. As long as those immediate customers were not being disrupted, life was good.

That perspective has to radically change. Every company must understand that their ultimate customers are the human beings who consume or use the products or services that their business provides or contributes to. I intentionally use the words *consumer* and *end user* instead of *customer* throughout this chapter to reinforce this critical distinction. Every so-called B2B (business to business) or industrial company must be as riveted to the end user as a retailer or consumer goods maker.

Microsoft had long been a traditional B2B company selling its software to computer makers, but under the leadership of CEO Satya Nadella, it has changed its mindset to focus on end users. The company still sells software tools directly to businesses, but now with a different perspective. Nadella and his team recognized that its products are used daily by thousands of human beings, so in many respects, Microsoft is a direct-to-consumer company. The sales force became the "customer success" team, charged with gathering a continuous flow of feedback from users and encouraged to discover new needs and new ways to make them more productive. Attitudes went from "we know it all" to "we have to learn what users really need."

That shift has changed Microsoft's product line and reignited its growth. As PCs declined, and with it, Microsoft's primary market, the company shifted its offerings to support mobile devices, connectivity, collaboration, visualization, and continuous innovation. It bet on three new technologies—AI, mixed reality (blending the physical world with virtual reality), and quantum computing—and created a range of tools customers can essentially rent or subscribe to, making them accessible to start-ups. The shift in perspective to end users reversed Microsoft's slowing growth and put it on a whole new trajectory.

Unless a company makes products for consumers, or sells directly to them, it probably spends little time dissecting that universe. Yet that's where the action is. That is where companies exhibit deep vulnerabilities, and also where huge opportunities lie. It's where consumer dissatisfaction festers and everyday problems go unnoticed. It is how companies and leaders can pick up clues—for example, from the unfettered communication that takes place on social media—about what consumers are unhappy with or what they are gravitating toward. The consumer is the ultimate source of ideas that can lead to years of exponential growth.

Some business leaders focus their decision-making on direct competitors. They track market share and dissect things like cost structure, brand recognition, distribution space, and the pricing power of the four or five companies that dominate their industry. Their energy goes toward making the products they make or the services they offer a little bit better. They tend to be product-centric and to rely on mass marketing and periodic advertising campaigns to spur demand.

As hard as it might be for people schooled in competitor-driven industry analysis to change their mindset, the linear sequential view of the value chain must shift 180 degrees, from competing to win customers at the next step in your value chain to learning about the end consumer:

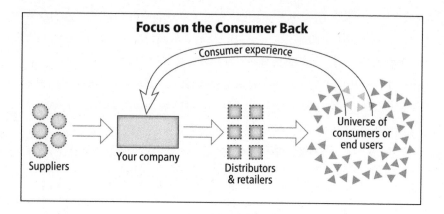

The digital giants relentlessly focus on the consumer's total experience and work backward. Amazon's Jeff Bezos instinctively—maybe compulsively—looks at things from the perspective of the consumer. He is constantly trying to improve things from that vantage point.

Anyone pitching a new initiative at Amazon has to begin the approval process with a six-page narrative document that explains what the consumer stands to gain (Amazon uses the term *customers*). The team drafts a press release and set of FAQs (frequently asked questions) that forces them to think through the benefits from the consumer's perspective—what problem it solves and how it will work for the consumer (the pricing, the technology behind it, what the disappointments might be, and the like)—before any work begins. Quantitative metrics for the required inputs and expected outcomes come later in the approval process.

The general principle of consumer focus is easy to accept at an online retailer like Amazon, but it applies to all the digital giants: Alphabet (Google's parent company), Facebook, Netflix, Twitter. The consumer experience drives everything they do, not the competition or their core competence. *How can we create a better consumer experience?* Competition matters only as it pertains to the consumer experience. How might other digital players change that experience and consumer expectations? Bezos makes his priority explicit: "When given the choice of obsessing over competitors or obsessing over customers, we always obsess over customers."

A focus on consumers gets exciting when you realize that technology and the Internet create so many new options for how to serve them. It is now possible to gather data about each individual consumer (Facebook has 2.3 billion of them) and to use that information to serve him or her better. My own shorthand for this idea is M=1, where M is a market segment and there's only one person in it.

Markets of One

M=1 is the ultimate in personalization. It is the foundation of competitive advantage that creates enormous value for the customer and shareholders at the same time.

As far back as the 1990s, Jeff Bezos predicted that his company would one day personalize a version of the website for each shopper based on that individual's preferences. Customized purchasing recommendations are now old hat, as are customized movie recommendations based on your personal viewing history. Consumers who are at first surprised by such customization quickly adapt to it and come to expect it.

What's different in the digital age is that a customized experience can be provided at the same or lower cost as one designed for a larger market segment. And in such cases, customization almost always wins. Apple's personalization is in its software. The choice of devices the company offers may be limited, but users can customize the features and choose applications to meet their individual needs.

We know that Starbucks caters to customers' preferences; it offers 170,000 possible beverage options at its stores, according to the company's website. Its use of data, sensors, the cloud, and artificial intelligence now allows it to engage with customers in an even more personalized way. It can send individualized messages to each of the 18.9 million people in its loyalty program. One member might get a message that reads "We think you'll love this new Menu Quest—designed just for you," while another might receive "It's a foggy day in SF. Warm up with our pumpkin spice latte!"

As Matt Ryan, Starbucks chief strategy officer, told the Boston Consulting Group team that helped build the company's personalization capability, "Previously, we sent e-mails to very large segments of customers. Now, we're able to do it on a very targeted basis, and what that allows us to do is to be more efficient and more effective with our communications so that we don't have to peanut butter a broad discount. We can go in more selectively and offer just what's right to get the next incremental level of engagement with us."

Technology is important, but the ultimate focus is on the consumer. As Gerri Martin-Flickinger, Starbucks executive vice president and chief technology officer, notes, "Everything we do in technology is centered around the customer connection in the store, the human connection, one person, one cup, one neighborhood at a time."

Lower cost also wins. One of Walmart's most important strategies in earlier decades was lowering the cost of logistics and increasing productivity, thereby making merchandise affordable by lots of low-income people. It was a great contribution to society. Its founder, Sam Walton, drove the company to focus on lower costs for the sake of the consumer. Today, digital technology and the Internet have made both low cost and personalization "must haves" for every consumer.

A legacy company conditioned to build a large market by creating something with mass appeal can completely miss the target. The key is to identify an experience that can both be personalized and appeal to a very large number of people, regardless of national or cultural boundaries.

To imagine an experience that can be personalized and will appeal to many people, start by thinking about an individual consumer experience. If you have spent your career in a functional area like production or finance that has no direct connection to the consumer, this may seem difficult. But consider an end-to-end experience in a person's life—for example, as they work, travel, socialize, shop, or seek medical care.

Dig in and get to know everything about a particular experience—say, buying a car or taking a vacation—through a combination of observation, analytics, reflection, and your own personal experience. Where are there points of friction or frustration? What are the touchpoints and pain points?

Mapping the "customer journey" is emerging as a distinct expertise. It involves breaking apart all of the interactions and decision steps a consumer goes through from first exposure to an idea or recognition of a need through to what happens after the person makes a purchase. I've seen some companies create a special team to do this work and to update and improve it continuously. Fidelity's Personal Investing unit put tremendous time and effort into mapping three key customer types and uses that knowledge to inform major decisions (see chapter 7 for more on this).

However sophisticated the data and methodology, analysis of the customer journey can only supplement, not fully replace, unfiltered observation of the consumer. Any small shopkeeper will tell you that watching customers and listening to their comments is crucial to making tactical decisions such as pricing and merchandise display. Even in the digital age, your edge depends in part on your ability to derive insights from what you observe.

Every leader and employee should look for opportunities to directly observe consumers and reflect on why their experience is the way it is. Why are people behaving that way or doing things the way they do? What is unsatisfactory to them? What might a consumer wish would happen differently? What is missing? Simple questions like these can generate powerful insights.

I find that leaders who develop their "observational acumen," the ability to notice things others miss, are often the ones who land on what a better consumer experience might look like. They imagine things consumers didn't even know they needed. Apple's Steve Jobs was famous for doing this.

Having worked with many senior leaders across the globe in almost all industries, I have found that there's a big deficit of observational acumen among the top ranks of many legacy companies. Over some fifty years I've had countless opportunities to meet with them informally, sometimes in their homes, in relaxed settings, where their priorities, interests, and skills came through loud and clear. But what also became clear is the gaping hole in their understanding of the consumer's end-to-end experience.

On the other hand, I saw Tadashi Yanai, the CEO of Japanese clothing company Fast Retailing, which includes brands such as Theory and Uniqlo, scour through his global business to handpick a team of people he sensed had a genuine feel for the consumer. He brought this group together and assigned them to go into the field as consumer anthropologists and reconvene to share their observations. Those collective insights gathered by relatively young and inexperienced employees guided decisions at Uniqlo at the highest levels of management. The CEO himself has superb instincts about consumers, and his focus and coaching foster a culture that values keen observation of consumers.

Kishore Biyani is the founder and CEO of Future Group,

one of India's largest retailers, which includes the Big Bazaar hypermarket chain, sometimes referred to as the Walmart of India. He also founded Pantaloons, which became India's largest clothing chain. Despite overseeing a retail empire, he makes it a point to observe consumers firsthand. "I'm on the floor twice a week," he once told me. "Whenever we go to meet with people, we go to stores, and we watch people. What are they putting in the shopping basket?"

When he noticed that girls in smaller villages were going to temple in jeans, he knew that social change was afoot. Shoppers were likely to be more receptive to Western clothing. And the new behavior suggested that girls were gaining respect and independence in their culture, and therefore might have more influence on purchase decisions. Biyani developed his observational acumen in an analog world, but it is even more important in the digital age.

As you think about how the consumer experience can be improved or even completely transformed, don't concern yourself with what your company is prepared to do about it. At least not yet. If you lock on to the things your company is already good at—your core competence—early on, you will almost surely constrain your imagination.

For almost forty years, the vast majority of companies have followed the tenet advocated by C. K. Prahalad and Gary Hamel, and later Chris Zook, to build on your core competence. That practice is now in question because it tends to focus people on the rearview mirror rather than the future. The digital giants have repeatedly demonstrated that in a world of fast-changing consumer behavior and consumer power, what you did yesterday may now be irrelevant. Companies flounder when their core competence becomes less relevant to the changing needs and tastes of the consumer. Others rise because they see something consumers will want, and believe they can use digital technology to do what has previously been impossible.

Even if your company lacks the capability to meet an unmet need, recognizing the opportunity can motivate you to find or build those capabilities. At the least, you will be able to anticipate how your industry or value chain might soon be disrupted, where you could fit in, and what must change.

Creating a 100x Future

I find that leaders in legacy companies have a hard time thinking big enough. They tend to settle for incremental improvement, but they shouldn't.

One way to create an entirely new market space is by combining pieces from existing industries. Where does an experience create frustration because the experience a consumer really wants requires connecting separate activities seamlessly and invisibly? Where should things be bundled together? Can the company create a new ecosystem and thereby transform the consumer experience in a way that satisfies a new need and ratchets up expectations?

You need a curious mind to ask the right questions, and observational acumen combined with imagination and basic knowledge of your business and algorithms to answer them. The skill, knowledge, and imagination needed to find those 100x market spaces doesn't have to reside in one person. As A. G. Lafley, former CEO of Procter & Gamble, has said, ideas can come from anywhere. Renowned consulting firm McKinsey & Company has begun to use hackathons in which a diverse group of people brainstorm to identify new opportunities.

Ultimately, the concept for a 100x market space has to gel into a mental picture of a consumer experience that can be transformed using technology, that can be customized and continuously improved through the use of data, and that will eventually generate lots of cash as it gets delivered at increasingly low incremental cost across multiple geographies.

We have seen investment bankers drive major improvements in moneymaking by connecting or disconnecting pieces of a value chain (vertical integration) or by merging companies to consolidate within an industry (horizontal integration). Those moves, typically aimed at reducing cost structures or controlling the most profitable part of a value chain, may be insightful, but they are rearranging things that already exist.

Leaders in the digital age take on a stiffer but more exhilarating challenge: to create something that does not yet exist and that *lots* of consumers will find desirable or necessary. Apple has so far sold 1.9 billion handsets, and the number of users is even greater. Netflix has 167 million registered subscribers worldwide as of January 2020 and a higher number of users. In India, some 500 million people now have access to mobile phones, and thanks to extremely low-cost usage rates spurred by Indian service provider Jio, e-commerce is taking off. The assumption behind the aggressive pursuit of big numbers is that profits will materialize later when gross margin turns exponentially upward. The race is to get to that upturn sooner.

Deciding which experiences you intend to provide depends in part on your assessment of how big that new market could actually be. The Internet is able to cross boundaries of geography, culture, and politics instantly. Digital technology makes the incremental cost of delivering that end-to-end experience to consumers close to zero. The business becomes a cash machine, and that cash can be used to further increase the market.

One way to stretch the imagination is by looking at things on a macro scale. Take Amazon, for example. Its revenues were about $220 billion in 2017. How much room does that leave for such a digital giant to grow? Consider that total global consumption is about $25 trillion—that's the sum of everything that people around the globe buy in a year. Online purchases accounted for about 10 percent of that sum in 2017, for a total of $2.5 trillion. The proportion of online sales is expected to grow. If e-commerce were to grow from 10 percent to 20 percent of total consumption, that would make it a $5 trillion market space. Viewed through this lens, Amazon is just getting started.

Amazon is hardly alone in doing this kind of big-picture thinking. I see it at Adobe, Netflix, Microsoft, and the other big e-commerce players. As competition among these

giants heats up, they will likely squeeze the slower, less ambitious, less aggressive legacy players.

My advice to leaders is to seek new big ideas by discussing with your team, with external experts, and with your
peers. Create a small group, being sure to include at least
one person who has command of algorithms and a nose for
customers, and some younger people who won't let the
conversation revert to past practices. Identify emerging
trends that are likely to be sustained for the next, say, ten
years. Demographic shifts are unstoppable once they're
under way, and while specific technological innovations
may be hard to predict, the general direction of technology,
computing speed, and innovation is not. For example, we
know to expect an uptick in the speed of innovation in
fields like medicine and materials science as artificial intelligence is further developed and applied.

Identify the Price Gap

No matter where you are in the current value chain, a laser
focus on the consumer is crucial for spotting a big opportunity for your company and potential disruption for others:
the price gap, the difference between the existing price to
the consumer and what the price *could be* if digital technology were creatively applied. Industries get overturned when
someone finds a way to exploit that gap for the benefit of
the consumer. Here is a generic diagram of where to find
the price gap:

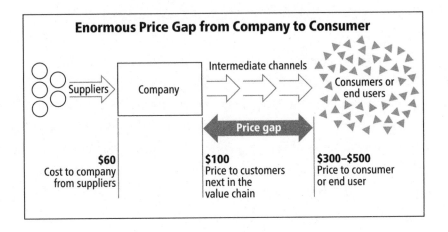

Enormous Price Gap from Company to Consumer

Suppliers › Company → Intermediate channels → Consumers or end users

Price gap

| **$60** Cost to company from suppliers | **$100** Price to customers next in the value chain | **$300–$500** Price to consumer or end user |

Say that it costs a publisher $7 to create a book, and a retailer like Barnes & Noble sells it for $30. The price gap here is $23. Amazon's Bezos sees those kinds of gaps as opportunities. Amazon's digital platform made it easy for a consumer to buy a book online, which would then be sent directly from a "fulfillment center" to the consumer's home. By eliminating the need for products to move from warehouses and distributors to far-flung retail shops, Amazon can shave several percentage points from the costs that would otherwise accumulate.

The price gap, measured in dollars, may point you toward an opportunity. But in a digital world, the consumer benefits compound. "Faster, cheaper, more convenient" is the oft-repeated catchphrase that describes the multiple advantages that a digitally enabled direct-to-consumer model offers to the consumer. That's why Amazon took such a fast and furious lead against traditional booksellers twenty years ago, a formula it has applied to many other categories ever since.

Digital companies do everything they can to connect with the end user directly. E-commerce entrepreneurs have rushed to fill direct-to-consumer niches in everything from mattresses (Casper) and suitcases (Away) to razors (Harry's) and socks (Bombas). When intermediaries get eliminated, costs are reduced. Consumers benefit from lower prices *as well as* more choice and greater convenience. The biggest winners strive to ensure that every partner in the ecosystem is also driving out excess cost and seeking to improve the overall consumer experience.

Competing in a Market Space

By creating a new market space, you force other companies to play your game. If you've created a more satisfying end-to-end consumer experience, others are forced to try to match it. And as they enter the fray, they will help expand the total market space. Since Disney launched Disney+, for example, the total number of subscribers to any streaming service and the total usage have increased.

The risk, of course, is that new competitors will redefine the game by bringing a different mix of capabilities to bear, again changing consumers' expectations. Despite the dominance of today's digital retail giants, for example, the dust has not yet settled. Amazon is experimenting with physical stores, as Walmart is feverishly expanding its presence online. E-commerce start-ups like Casper and Away have opened stores in select cities so consumers can touch and feel their products, and Harry's now sells its razors at Target to reach customers who don't like to shop on the Internet.

While industry experts debate the merits of all the new players in video streaming, each of the big contenders has a different blend of assets. Disney can complement its Disney+ video service with theme parks, books, toys, digital games, and apps created around its characters and stories. WarnerMedia has movie studios and HBO, Apple has devices and software, while Netflix is purely a streaming service with the ability to create content. The crucial question, however, remains unanswered: What experience will the consumer prefer?

New entrants can affect pricing, as well. In the pre-digital days, new products created new market spaces that generally took years to mature. Take DRAMs (dynamic random access memory chips), which at one time were a wholly new invention and market space. Over time, competitors entered, supply outpaced demand, the whole industry got commoditized, and profitability plummeted. It is possible that the streaming wars will create a similar scenario where supply outstrips demand, resulting in a drop in prices and profitability. Some digital market spaces could see profitability fall as quickly as the market has expanded. E-commerce in India is a case in point. The recent expansion has largely been driven by three digital players: Amazon, Flipkart (majority owned by Walmart), and a new deep-pocketed player, Reliance Industries. Reliance owns telecommunications carrier Jio and a large retail chain. In early 2020 it launched JioMart, its e-commerce site. Alibaba has a growing presence in India, as well.

In the race for global dominance, India has become a crucial battleground among these juggernauts. With more Indians using mobile phones and multiple players aggressively trying to make the online shopping experience convenient and appealing, the market space is primed to expand. The fight for customers will intensify. These companies know that customer acquisition is costly but absolutely key, and that profits might not materialize for a while.

Each of the giants is looking for an edge. Recognizing that a growing number of new users live in smaller towns, for example, Amazon set up fifteen thousand locations across the country where people could get assistance navigating Amazon's website. It simplified the mobile app so it drew less battery power. And it created an app in Hindi, the most popular language in India.

Flipkart, a local upstart, was founded in 2007 by two former Amazon employees. It was fueled by multiple rounds of fundraising, including $2.5 billion from Soft-Bank's Vision Fund, to become India's largest e-commerce company. Then Walmart bought a 77 percent stake in Flipkart for $16 billion, a move Walmart CEO Doug McMillon saw as the fastest way to enter the burgeoning market. To concentrate their efforts in India, Walmart withdrew from Brazil and the U.K.

A pricing war had already broken out when an unexpected force—the Indian government—intervened. Under pressure from small vendors, the government restricted foreign companies from owning inventory. Non-Indian companies also had to drop the practice of offering discounts and exclusives to select customers. The new rules tilted the game toward Reliance's new venture, which is geared toward linking with the mom-and-pop shops that are prevalent throughout India.

The participants are accelerating the market expansion in India. Revenue from e-commerce in India is expected to grow from $39 billion in 2017 to $120 billion in 2020, an annual rate of 51 percent, the highest in the world. One could argue that all of the e-commerce players will benefit from the expansion, but only time will tell which way customers will skew and whether intense competition among digital giants will cause profitability to decline across the space.

What is needed to serve each individual customer, anytime, anyplace, billions of times every day? Algorithms! The next chapter shows why a digital platform of artificial intelligence and machine learning algorithms is now the centerpiece of any company's competitive advantage.

CHAPTER 4

DIGITAL PLATFORMS AT THE CENTER OF THE BUSINESS

Rule #2: Algorithms and data are essential weapons.

You will not be able to create a superior end-to-end experience that is personalized for each individual *and* at scale unless you are prepared to make algorithms and data central to your business. There is simply no way around this reality.

All of today's digital giants have a digital platform—a set of algorithms stitched together to collect and process data—at the core of their business. Most companies that were digitally born started with a simple version of their digital platform and improved it over time.

Even Alibaba, whose founder, Jack Ma, did not have a background in computer science or writing software, was built on a foundation of algorithms to gather, process, and transmit digital information. In 1997 Ma saw an opportunity to use the Internet to facilitate transactions between buyers and suppliers of industrial goods, for which Alibaba would collect a fee. His seventeen-member start-up team included software engineers and coders with skills in computer science and Java programming. The company's exponential growth, from zero to a market value of $450 billion in 2019, has been based on enhancing its original digital platform and creating new platforms such as Tmall for e-commerce and Alipay for electronic payments.

A digital platform in and of itself is not an enduring competitive advantage, but not having one is a competitive *disadvantage* given everything it enables a company to do. A digital platform is what fuses an ecosystem together, directs and analyzes the data that flows to and from a large number of sources, and customizes the end-to-end consumer experience. It enables new moneymaking models, can detect patterns in consumer behavior, and can make predictions with all sorts of implications for efficiency and growth.

Digital Capabilities vs. a Digital Platform

Leaders of some legacy companies are quick to boast that their company is building its digital capability. What they really mean is that the company is using algorithms to improve some of its internal processes, or has built a separate online sales channel. Those efforts can generate cost benefits and preserve some sales the physical stores are losing, but they fall far short of the benefits the digital giants achieve.

In countering Amazon's ever-expanding reach, for example, many department store chains like Macy's and JCPenney created websites so customers could shop online. Their e-commerce businesses were basically tacked on to their core businesses and run in parallel. The retailers did not transform their logistics and in most cases did not fundamentally change the consumer's shopping experience. Their moneymaking models remained essentially the same. Profits got squeezed, precipitating several rounds of store closings.

The coronavirus pandemic caught many traditional retailers technologically unprepared for the sudden shift in consumer behavior and desperately short of cash. Platform-based companies like Amazon could step up to meet consumers' needs, and legacy retailers like Walmart whose digital platforms were further along were able to adapt quickly.

It's no secret that both Amazon and Walmart have been experimenting to find a combination of digital and physical that serves consumers best. And as noted in the previous chapter, smaller e-commerce companies like Casper, Away, and Harry's now have physical stores. Whether or not physical outlets are included in the mix, having a digital platform and access to the data it generates must be central to how the business serves customers, operates, and makes money. Legacy companies have a decision to make: build a digital platform, piecemeal or all at once; buy one, as Walmart did with Jet.com and Disney did with Hulu; or join someone else's, as many smaller retailers and some large consumer goods companies have done, by using third-party platforms such as Shopify.

Acquiring the necessary technology is getting easier and less expensive, so it should not be seen as a barrier. There's no need to hire armies of technologists to build new systems from scratch. Algorithms can be bought and reverse engineered, and computing power, data storage, and even algorithmic capability is available in the cloud.

In 2013, Piyush Gupta, CEO of Singapore's DBS Bank, saw how quickly digital companies like Alibaba had taken hold of online payments and lending, and knew DBS had to change. The bank had a clear path to grow revenues by serving more small and medium-size businesses, but profit margins would be nowhere near what the digital players had. Gupta concluded that DBS had to build a digital platform and put it at the core of the business. "It's not just having a bunch of apps," he explained. "It is rethinking the technology architecture."

Gupta had observed how quickly even his elderly parents had adapted to the Internet, and believed people in the company could change as well. To reinforce the company's transformation, he and his team changed the frame of reference. They talked about the organization as a technology company, not a bank, and compared themselves to tech companies instead of to financial firms like Morgan Stanley.

My friend Krishna Sudheendra, CEO of UST, remembers talking with Piyush Gupta at a business gathering organized by a sovereign wealth fund. Sudheendra told him that he had just been talking with some of Gupta's competitors. "Oh really, which ones?" Gupta asked. "People from Citigroup and Bank of America," Sudheendra replied.

Gupta quickly corrected him: "Those are not my competitors. My competitors are Google, Amazon, Alibaba, and Tencent."

In 2018, *Global Finance* named DBS "The Best Bank in the World"—an award based on performance over the past year as well as other criteria including reputation, management excellence, and leadership in digital transformation. That same year, DBS was named the world's best digital bank by *Euromoney*, which noted that DBS had begun to be valued as a digital company.

Leaders of other companies should take note. Understanding the power of a digital platform at the center of your business is now as essential as understanding supply chains and corporate finance.

What a Digital Platform Really Is

A digital platform is a set of algorithms that collect and analyze data. Each algorithm is a specific sequence of steps for solving a problem. It is a software version of what our brains do automatically. Human beings store data in whatever crude form we receive it and use it for decisions like making a prediction.

For example, in India, where my family ran a shoe shop when I was growing up, we had to make predictions about the demand for shoes. There are four seasons in India, the most difficult being the rainy season. During the rainy season, one festival created peak demand. A period when most weddings took place also created significant demand. We had to decide how many pairs of shoes to buy, of what size and color. Overbuying was not an option, because if the inventory sat around it would collect moisture and rot. Inventory also tied up our cash, a crucial concern given that local borrowing costs were typically 24 percent per annum.

With no radios or newspapers, let alone computers, to keep us informed, we rode our bicycles to villages four miles out to talk to farmers about how the crops were doing, and we speculated about the timing and duration of the rainy season. We relied on our brains to use the historical data to make predictions based on the probabilities of multiple factors. My brothers and I had a running competition to see who would be more accurate. With more data over time, our predictions improved.

In doing that, we were living and breathing Bayes' theorem, a mathematical rule invented by Reverend Thomas Bayes in 1763 and used in most digital platforms today. If you know the probability of an occurrence from past data and you integrate new information, Bayes' theorem can predict the probability of the event happening in the future. This principle is used in every mathematical model used to make predictions and is at the heart of the Gallup polls.

Algorithms now go beyond sticking to prescribed mechanical steps. Those that replicate more complex thought processes, such as recognizing patterns in written words and images, reasoning, and comparing alternative responses, fall into the realm of artificial intelligence. Machine learning, a subset of artificial intelligence, describes algorithms designed to improve their own output based on experience doing the task. These algorithms are used for things such as speech recognition and online fraud detection. My point is that a platform of algorithms is not as mysterious as it seems. Businesspeople don't have to invent the algorithms, they just need to know what they are and what they can do. That knowledge will open the aperture of the mind and instill the belief that something that could not be done in the past now can be done.

Take Google. In the late 1990s, cofounders Larry Page and Sergey Brin developed the aptly named PageRank algorithm that powers its search engine. Until then, Internet searches gave results based on how many times a search term appeared, regardless of the context. PageRank made it possible to sort results based on the item's linkages to other pages and the quality of those pages, or their "authority," as John MacCormick, associate professor of computer science at Dickinson College, puts it. PageRank generated more relevant search results than the existing alternatives and was key to the company's phenomenal success.

Combining and refining algorithms over time helps a company build competitive advantage. Google is continuously making changes to its algorithms, both frequent incremental improvements and occasional big ones. In 2018, it made 3,234 improvements to Google Search, according to Google's website. And in October 2019, it announced a new algorithm that promises to return better results for one out of ten queries. As Rob Copeland reported in *The Wall Street Journal,* Google "harnessed advanced machine learning and mathematical modeling to produce better answers to complex search queries and questions that often confound its current algorithm." Google believes the new sequence of code—called Bidirectional Encoder Representations from Transformers, or BERT—is among the largest improvements to search in half a decade.

Amazon's algorithms have never been static. Early in the company's life, it used software that it bought from a spin-off of MIT's Media Lab. Customers had to rate a few dozen books, and based on that, the algorithm would recommend some others. But as Brad Stone describes in his book, *The Everything Store,* founder Jeff Bezos thought this process was too much work for the consumer to go through. So he asked a handful of computer scientists on his team to come up with something better.

Within a few weeks they created an algorithm that made recommendations based on what books customers had already purchased. It was an early demonstration of serving customers in an individualized way. As Stone writes, that algorithm, called Similarities, was "the seed that would grow into Amazon's formidable personalization effort." In the many years since then, Amazon has greatly increased its ranks of computer scientists, who continually create, refine, and enhance its algorithms.

Many algorithms are not proprietary. Today any business has access to algorithms from companies such as Algorithmia that have arisen to meet that need. The computing power needed to store and process data is now available in the cloud at variable cost. Even when AI researchers work for a private company, some of them follow an ethos to share their work with other computer scientists. They demand publication of at least parts of their algorithms as a condition of their employment. These developments are driving what some refer to as the democratization of computer science.

A company's competitive edge depends not only on the technology itself but also on the selection of algorithms and data. Netflix no longer depends solely on its streaming technology to set it apart. That capability can be built, as Disney has done with Disney+. The same is true for digital platforms themselves. I have seen several large companies build a digital platform using a combination of proprietary and off-the-shelf software with fewer than a dozen people in less than a year.

Walmart's approach was to *buy* a digital platform. It acquired Jet.com in 2016 for $3.3 billion. Walmart had dabbled in e-commerce starting in the early 2000s, but by 2008, it still ranked just thirteenth in Internet sales, far short of Amazon. Opening Walmart.com to third-party sellers in 2009 increased revenue, but not enough. Doug McMillon, who became Walmart CEO in 2014, saw the acquisition of Jet.com as a way to light the fire. With the acquisition came some very advanced algorithms for dynamic pricing, as well as the technology expertise Walmart needed. McMillon put Jet.com CEO Marc Lore and his team in charge of Walmart's U.S. e-commerce platform, and Walmart's online revenues began to move. In 2018, although still far behind Amazon, Walmart rated third in overall U.S. e-commerce sales.

Some traditional companies have found the prospect of building their own platform to reach the end consumer too daunting, too expensive, or just plain unnecessary. Canada-based Shopify was created to satisfy that need. It reported having some eight hundred thousand companies using its platform in the fall of 2019.

What a Platform Can Do

Questions about what you want a digital platform to do are just as important as questions about how to go about creating one. Trying to convert an existing business to a digital platform all at once is high risk. A "big bang" approach can easily overwhelm the organization and damage the core business, which is likely generating the cash needed to fund the new initiatives. On the other hand, a piecemeal approach to creating a digital platform can both fail to close the gap with online competitors and fail to produce any real competitive advantage.

Companies need expert advice to answer the important questions, such as whether to start a digital platform separately or to build a simple one on top of existing systems. Vendors exist to help create new systems and bypass issues related to SAP or ERP or inadequate IT infrastructure. Also, start-ups have arisen to provide pretrained AI models and curated data sets or to provide drag-and-drop software modules so that in-house computer scientists don't have to build them.

TensorFlow, for example, is an open-source platform of tools, libraries, and other resources built to support machine learning. Google initially built it for its own use, for implementing products like Search, Gmail, and Google

Maps. But TensorFlow is now an open system that anyone can access, and many companies do, including Airbnb, LinkedIn, PayPal, Lenovo, and GE. PayPal, for example, uses TensorFlow to detect patterns of fraud. It is one of many tools available through Google Open Source.

The real impact of digital technology, though, depends on combining knowledge of what technology can do and business judgment about how to use it. Great ideas often come from a handful of people with different kinds of expertise working closely together. Envisioning the consumer experience and the market, the ecosystem, and the kinds of data you want to use for what purpose—these are decisions human beings must make.

Conceptualizing the platform will be easier if you think about its many sources of competitive power. The ability to personalize an end-to-end consumer experience, create market spaces of 100x, and match supply and demand as Uber, Lyft, and Didi Chuxing do are now familiar ones. But there are others.

The ability to lower costs by eliminating intermediaries is important. But an equally powerful benefit of a digital platform is the ability to make price changes instantly, frequently, and in highly targeted ways. Pricing based on minute-by-minute information that comes through a company's digital platform is especially tough for physical competitors to beat.

Dynamic pricing makes it possible to adjust prices for local markets and in some cases for individual consumers. It can undercut competitors and is powerful protection against inventory obsolescence and sudden spikes in the price of commodities.

Amazon was perhaps *too* good at picking up discrepancies when a third-party retailer on its Marketplace listed the same product elsewhere at a lower price. It required third parties to offer the same or lower price on its site, ostensibly to protect the Amazon shopper, or the third party could be booted off Marketplace. Of course, these comparisons and adjustments were happening at computer speed. Third-party retailers protested Amazon's algorithm-driven pricing policy, saying it unfairly forced them to drop their prices, putting their profit margins at risk. As a remedy, in summer 2019 Amazon introduced a program called Sold by Amazon, which set pricing guidelines aimed at protecting a seller's profit margin.

As the digital giants use dynamic pricing to outmaneuver their competition, they never lose sight of the consumer. Amazon, for example, is known for its ruthless efficiency in getting products from the supplier to the consumer. Its commitment to the consumer has led it to pass along the benefit in the form of lower prices rather than take fatter margins.

This principle is so deeply rooted and widely acknowledged that when CVS and Aetna merged in 2018, some analysts speculated that any cost improvement from combining the two companies' pharmacy benefits management operations would have to be passed on to consumers. Why? Because Amazon had just entered the pharmaceutical industry by buying PillPack, an online pharmacy, and it was understood that Amazon would use the efficiency of its direct-to-consumer model to lower prices.

A digital platform is also the key to exponential growth. For one thing, the data it gathers can point to opportunities for a new consumer experience that can be delivered by the existing platform. As I discussed in chapter 3, data already collected about the individual consumer makes it possible to meet yet another need in the person's total life experience with great accuracy and without the costs associated with acquiring the customer.

As a result, revenues increase, as does gross margin, because the cost of getting that additional revenue is incrementally small. Add to that the benefit of using data and algorithms to analyze new offerings and guide targeted improvements in each iteration and you also reduce the risk of innovation.

Many born-digital companies have shown us how quickly they can create multiple streams of revenue and increase gross margins using the same basic platform. Amazon has expanded its sources of revenues based on the same digital platform to include direct sales, third-party sales, advertising, and loans.

Qantas Airlines, a traditional company that was reborn digital, used its digital platform to create a new revenue stream in an area far afield from booking travel. It discovered that the platform it used for engaging with the travelers who were part of its rewards program could be used to meet another need they had: health insurance. Those who buy health insurance through Qantas earn travel points, and healthy behaviors such as walking earn them even more points.

But perhaps the greatest source of power from a digital platform is its ability to support entirely new and different moneymaking models. Uber, Lyft, Didi Chuxing, and other digital companies provide products and services based on complex calculations that would be virtually impossible to process without algorithms. With the same digital platform, they are now expanding into new services and sources of revenue, such as food delivery.

Adobe Systems, known for software products like Acrobat Reader and Photoshop, used a digital platform and cloud storage to turn its product into a service. Instead of selling software on a disk or licensing it to be downloaded for a multimillion-dollar onetime fee, it created a digital platform that allowed users to pay a subscription fee for access to the software products they needed. Periodic as-you-go payments freed customers from having to make a large investment up front.

Customers welcomed the option of subscribing to use Adobe's software and choosing the options that met their individual needs. The new moneymaking model made the products more affordable, which is especially important for cash-strapped start-ups, and meant the product would always be up to date. It reversed Adobe's slowing growth, exploding the size of the market. Between 2015 and 2019, revenues more than doubled and market value increased from $40 billion to $160 billion.

Adobe was early in a larger trend pioneered by other

software companies to turn software into a service. The acronym SaaS is now common, as are its many variations, including, for example, DaaS—Disney as a service, which Matthew Ball, sage media expert, venture partner, and former head of strategy at Amazon Studios, coined to describe what he saw as Disney's emerging business model.

Alibaba's Platform-Driven Global Expansion

In the hands of imaginative leaders, digital platforms present almost infinite opportunities for new sources of revenue growth. Amazon found that the digital infrastructure it was using to support third-party sellers on its Marketplace could be an entirely new customer offering. Andy Jassy, who was running that part of the business, had the idea back in 2006 to make its capability available to other companies for a fee. That was the origin of AWS (Amazon Web Services), which brought in $25.7 billion in revenues in 2018 and is now the company's most profitable unit.

While Jassy developed and pitched the service for what he believed would be a huge new market space, he insisted on downplaying its profitability, in order to hold off would-be competitors. That worked for a while, but Google, Microsoft, IBM, and Alibaba have since jumped in. AWS had nearly half the market share for cloud computing, or Infrastructure as a Service, in 2018. And while the total market space continues to expand, heavyweight competitors are growing fast and competition is fierce.

According to Gartner, Inc., Alibaba Cloud experienced the strongest growth among the leading vendors, growing 92.6 percent from 2017 to 2018. Gartner noted that Alibaba Cloud achieved that growth by tapping into an ecosystem of independent companies that provided infrastructure and software services. That arrangement preserves its financial capability to continue to invest heavily in R&D and continue its global expansion.

Alibaba has expanded its range of offerings as broadly and quickly as Amazon and elicits the same kind of trepidation among competitors when it makes a new move. While the two companies overlap in terms of markets, they are not exactly parallel. Alibaba's initial foray into the online world was providing a platform to connect smaller suppliers with industrial buyers. Later it added Taobao, which connected individuals who wanted to sell something with individuals who wanted to buy, more like eBay than Amazon. Later it added Tmall, an e-commerce platform akin to Amazon, and Tmall Global, to do the same across country boundaries. Along the way it created Alipay, a digital payment system, which has since become part of Ant Financial, an umbrella for payments and financial services.

The company is organized into teams that support different sets of customers, with three shared layers of digital technology. As Arthur Yeung and Dave Ulrich explain in *Reinventing the Organization,* the first technology layer comprises the various systems needed to support everyday work, such as procurement and customer outreach. The third layer is IT infrastructure, which handles routine processes, security, and data storage.

The middle layer is the digital platform at the core of the company, which creates tremendous value for Alibaba and its partners. It combines data from across the ecosystem and uses algorithmic tools to create a 360-degree view of the consumer that is constantly updated. This layer includes technology that identifies "the commonality in data and technology requirements of all businesses and turns these common requirements into standardized service modules to be used by teams like merchant management, user management, shopping cart, payment, search, and security."

Alibaba leverages that middle platform to attract new partners and help existing partners succeed. It offers a unique proposition to sizable companies, which goes something like this: "Here is our plug-and-play platform; we will work with you to connect with our analytic tools and to allow data to flow back and forth." The local partners can combine data Alibaba has collected along with their own, from online and physical stores, and use analytic tools on the platform to target the market more precisely, get a fuller picture of the consumer, make personalized recommendations, and otherwise serve customers better and grow their business.

The more digital capabilities Alibaba builds and the more data it amasses, the more desirable it is for outside companies to connect to its digital platform. What's especially unusual in Alibaba's approach is that it takes an equity stake in some of those partners, so the relationships are cemented and the benefits of growth are shared. For example, it co-funded delivery and tracking company

Cainiao in 2013 and expanded its equity stake in 2017. And it has a 40 percent stake in ShopRunner, a subscription two-day delivery service.

The Central Role of Data

Alibaba's promise of access to a vast amount of data from which companies can create a full picture of the consumer is a tantalizing opportunity. Securing a flow of data to and from the right sources is an important part of a company's competitive advantage. The quality, reliability, and timing of data are crucial to the speed and quality of a company's decisions, whether the algorithms do the deciding or provide information to support human judgment.

You have to ensure that the data you need flows freely and can be made compatible. Depending on what you use it for, you may need a ton of it. Machine learning and artificial intelligence generate higher-quality outputs when they have more data to "learn" from. This is particularly true for advanced applications such as autonomous vehicles. In fact, the need for huge quantities of data to represent the many varied situations cars must navigate is one of the reasons companies seeking to provide mobility in one form or another have been forming such extensive ecosystems.

Much of the data in the emerging mobility ecosystems is generated by sensors in the vehicles themselves. In the Internet of Things, sensors are built into all kinds of machinery to collect data in real time for all sorts of purposes. GE uses sensors on its turbines, for example, to help predict when the parts are due for routine maintenance. Similarly, Schindler uses data from sensors embedded in its elevators to predict and diagnose equipment failures.

Whether data is gathered by sensors or interaction with customers, the digital platform must be designed to capture it at precisely the right points. While Amazon's engagement with customers is well known, the company gathers data from critical points in its operations as well, such as the point where the box is sealed and ready to be shipped. Access to the right data, filtered through the right algorithms, allows for fast responses, whether automated or not. It enables speed and efficiency in innovation by allowing "minimum viable product" ideas to go through experimentation and iterations quickly.

In forging its healthcare ecosystem (which I address at length in the next chapter), Apple is trying to overcome two of the biggest barriers to the flow of data in healthcare: government regulation and a hodgepodge of formats. It is aiming to reconcile data that comes from different entities, including health insurance, labs, hospitals, clinics, and physicians, and encrypt it. It also encrypts the data that comes directly from an individual's Health app or Watch, giving the consumer control over how it is used.

Much of Apple's technology efforts are invisible to outsiders, but smoothing the flow of data promises to improve healthcare delivery overall. Tim Cook and his team at Apple must have charted the flow of data as they were developing their thinking about the healthcare ecosystem: from an individual's Health app to insurance companies and from the insurer to the individual in the form of reduced rates and fitness incentives; from the individual's Health app to the physician and from the physician to the individual to revise treatment plans; from aggregated data to a research institution and from a research institution to patients involved in drug trials.

Acquiring data is a challenge for start-ups, because they are still building their customer base. Data can be bought from third parties, but it's expensive. Legacy companies have copious amounts of data, but it is often buried in silos, formatted inconsistently, and incomplete. Today vendors can create a single version of the data rather inexpensively, in some cases for less than a million dollars.

Those challenges can be thought through by posing basic questions: What data do we need? What data do we have? How complete is it? Is it captured in the right form?

Alibaba found opportunity in data it already had access to: the transactions sellers made on its platform. With a seller's permission, Alibaba could tap that data to assess things like how well the seller's business was doing and whether its partners had good credit ratings. Algorithms could then predict its creditworthiness in real time and greatly reduce the risk in microlending to small companies. That concept was the basis for Ant Financial, which Alibaba launched in 2012.

The need to store massive amounts of data raises the question of whether to store it yourself or use a cloud service. Bear in mind that if your business succeeds, the amount of data and the cost of storing it will increase exponentially.

Consumers can get great value from a company's use of

data and algorithms. But that value will quickly disappear if privacy or security is compromised. Thus far consumers generally have been satisfied with the exchange of data for better service or free usage. They readily sign off on the lengthy terms-of-service agreements that come with the use of many websites. But consumers expect companies to secure their personal information and respect their privacy. Data breaches send customers scurrying, and advertising that is *too* spot-on raises concerns. Even the algorithms themselves have come under fire for codifying and, through machine learning, amplifying human biases in activities ranging from extending credit and screening job applicants to fighting crime.

As data permeates our everyday lives, protecting it and using it appropriately becomes a weighty responsibility. The adoption of autonomous vehicles will surely be stymied if the computer systems governing their every move are susceptible to hacking. Healthcare ecosystems will be disrupted if the exchange of medical records is not secure.

With history as a guide, we can assume that where there is a problem, someone somewhere is working on a solution. In 2019 Google released a set of tools to help companies protect customers' personal data, and some experts contend that data stored in the cloud is better protected against cyberattacks than data stored on individual company servers.

Apple has long held that privacy is one of its central values, and its emphasis on personal privacy may prove to be an advantage in the current context. As the company moves into healthcare, Apple is using a "federated" computing model that keeps data on individuals' devices rather than in the cloud, and applies encryption technology and other security measures to protect access to that data.

If the digital giants break trust with consumers yet retain their power, regulators will step in. The European Union has already passed rules regarding how companies store, process, and share data. U.S. regulators and legislators will do the same. Some lawmakers have proposed making the source code in algorithms available to the public as a check on potential biases. The Indian government has deemed that data is public property that all can use with specified constraints. Meanwhile, a growing number of towns and states have prohibited the use of facial recognition because of concerns about inherent biases and privacy. And when people learned that Facebook had shared users' personal data with British political consulting firm Cambridge Analytica, public criticism was scorching, and Congress held hearings that put CEO Mark Zuckerberg in the hot seat. Digital giants may face restrictions, but they won't disappear. Nor will their watchdogs.

B2W Digital's Platform-Based Expansion

Traditional companies that are overwhelmed by the prospect of building a business around a digital core should look to companies that have done it. Fidelity Personal Investing, a prominent example in chapter 7, is one example. Lojas Americanas, Brazil's largest retailer, is another.

It was in the late 1990s, just a few years after Amazon

first started selling books online, when leaders at the Brazilian brick-and-mortar retail company recognized the tremendous potential of giving customers the option to shop online. They laid the seeds for what would become a separate company and digital giant in its own right: B2W, a publicly traded company whose market value in January 2020 was R$37 billion (U.S. $8.5 billion), making it one of the thirty most valuable companies on the Brazilian stock exchange.

Online shopping was just emerging in Brazil, as it was elsewhere in the world, when Lojas Americanas created its e-commerce platform, Americanas.com. It would offer products such as clothing, linens, leather goods, and cellphones that were complementary to the small home appliances, candy, toys, health and personal care products, and underwear that were sold at the physical stores.

No one knew much about digital shopping platforms at the time, but Lojas found people with expertise to build the platform, and it quickly found its place as a leader in the nascent market. So did another player, Submarino, an e-commerce start-up that launched around the same time offering merchandise as well as online ticketing, travel, and consumer credit. The e-commerce market was untapped, so there was plenty of room for both Americanas.com and Submarino to grow quickly, and they did. They dominated the market space, even as a bevy of e-commerce start-ups began to enter.

In 2005–06, the e-commerce players began to consolidate. Americanas.com bought the third-largest e-commerce player, Shoptime, which also had a home shopping TV channel. And the following year, it merged with Submarino.

At the time of the merger, Miguel Gutierrez, CEO of Lojas Americanas, and Carlos Alberto Sicupira, its chairman, decided it made sense for the e-commerce business to be run as a separate entity. That's when B2W was created, with Anna Saicali, formerly the head of technology at Americanas.com, as its CEO. Lojas Americanas retained a majority stake (53.25 percent) in B2W, and the remaining shares began trading on the Brazilian stock exchange in August 2007.

B2W was born as the largest e-commerce company in Latin America, encompassing multiple brands and operations on separate digital platforms. As Saicali set out to integrate them, the global financial crisis erupted, putting all investments on hold. "We didn't know what would happen in the world economy or how Brazil would be affected," Saicali recalls. "So while we were selling a lot and had this great opportunity ahead of us, we said 'No more capital investment.' We had to focus on conserving cash."

That stance allowed B2W to weather the crisis unscathed. The company generated a profit, distributed dividends, and even bought back shares during that period. By 2010 the company was resuming work on its platform when it hit another major roadblock. This one, though, became a catalyst for B2W to change its strategy and build a stronger, broader, digital platform at its center.

Throughout its life, B2W had relied on outside distributors and logistics companies to deliver its goods. Other on-line sellers did, too, and their number had exploded as virtually every big retailer in Brazil decided they needed an e-commerce presence. The problem was that the distributors and logistics infrastructure had not kept pace with the rise in e-commerce traffic. When orders peaked during Christmas of 2010, the third parties simply could not deliver. Customers were devastated, and B2W, being the country's largest e-commerce company, got the lion's share of the complaints.

That event caused Saicali and her team to take a step back. Customers must come first, they affirmed, and everything they did had to reflect that clear priority. So along with building the business around a customer-facing digital platform, the team concluded that B2W had to build its own logistics and distribution infrastructure.

Those three items—technology, logistics/distribution, and customer experience—became the pillars of a three-year strategic plan that triggered a new investment cycle that topped $1 billion.

B2W's leaders knew where they were headed and what steps they had to take to get there, but the cash situation was concerning. B2W was selling goods it kept in its inventories, just as its brick-and-mortar parent Lojas Americanas had always done. As its growth accelerated after the financial crisis, more and more cash was tied up in inventory.

In discussing cash usage at one board meeting, Saicali proposed a solution: Allow other sellers, who would hold their own inventory, to use B2W's digital platform to sell their goods; B2W would collect a commission on those sales. I was present at that meeting. The idea sparked a lively discussion that concluded with the board giving Saicali the go-ahead. In 2013, the company launched B2W Marketplace, a two-sided platform connecting buyers and third-party sellers. Cash still was negative—and would be for several years before a projected sharp upturn—as the company built its future, but third-party sales helped ease the situation.

Progress on the new strategic plan did not go unnoticed. Tech investment firm Tiger Global had been tracking B2W and was won over by B2W's vision and execution in the first year. In 2014 it announced its intention to invest $1 billion at an 85 percent premium over B2W's current stock price. The company's shareholders fully supported the investment, and the funding allowed the company to accelerate its next steps.

B2W acquired three companies in quick succession that gave it a robust logistics platform, a network of storage facilities and transit hubs, and a carrier service that had already been serving e-commerce customers. No more Christmas blackouts!

Building the third strategic pillar, technology capabilities, took a multipronged effort. Throughout B2W's life, Saicali had made a point of keeping abreast of emerging trends and capabilities in technology. With a clear view of how central a digital platform is to ensuring a positive customer experience, she made it her personal mission to make B2W a world-class technology company. New capabilities would come from a combination of organic growth of the tech team, acquisitions of tech companies, and structured collaborations with leading technology experts.

B2W made eleven acquisitions in two years, each of which added an important kind of technology expertise. These included three systems development companies— Uniconsult, Ideais, and Tarkena—which tackled back-office systems, front-office systems, and customer data and inventory management, respectively. Those three deals doubled the existing in-house team to a total of more than six hundred engineers and prompted the creation of a center for innovation and entrepreneurship. Admatic brought specialized tools for things like price comparisons and optimizing virtual stores. E-smart was a developer of platform technology for creating online stores. Other acquisitions had expertise in artificial intelligence, online security, integration of online and offline stores, and selling on Instagram.

To tackle specific technology challenges, Saicali made the rounds to MIT, Stanford, Harvard, and consulting firms in search of experts who could give advice. She created collaboration programs with labs at those and other top institutions, including some in Latin America.

By 2017, the B2W digital platform encompassed e-commerce, inventory management, and logistics for its own product offerings as well as those from third parties. The company, which had been a consumer of cash for most of its life, became a cash generator. Having reached her goal of making the company cash positive by 2019, Saicali handed the CEO job to her successor, and she became chair.

Still, 2017 was not a stopping point. The digital platform, accumulation of data, technology capabilities, and solid financial footing became the base for more innovation. For example, B2W created Ame, a platform-based digital wallet for mobile phones—a one-stop app for financial services or general services. It also made a contractual agreement with Lojas Americanas for consumers to order online and pick up merchandise at a store. Along the way, the company kept sharpening its focus, streamlining the product mix and divesting some things such as online ticketing.

Using data for decision-making became even more potent with the support of artificial intelligence. The combination of copious amounts of data and advanced capabilities to process it allows B2W to understand consumer behavior, support the merchandise buyers, and know its own people better. As Saicali says, "We use big data for everything here, in all the domains, and to help make all decisions." She adds, "It is possible only because we have a very digital mindset."

B2W's efforts over decades and through numerous challenges pushed B2W's market value from a tiny R$3.4 billion (about U.S. $1.5 billion) at its creation in 2006 to R$32.9 billion (about U.S. $8 billion) by the end of 2019. It has remained far ahead of Amazon, which first entered Latin America in 2013, and Walmart, which has both a physical and online presence there.

B2W started its digital efforts early in the digital age, but its commitment to its customers and willingness to use cash to build the necessary technology capabilities are examples every company should follow.

Leaders have to constantly innovate to incorporate relevant new technologies into their digital platforms, especially to connect with ecosystem partners. The next chapter describes how an ecosystem is a competitive advantage and an indispensable ingredient for a profitable cash-generating business.

CHAPTER 5

═══════════

VALUE-CREATING ECOSYSTEMS

Rule #3: A company does not compete. Its ecosystem does.

Are you afraid that your company will be overtaken by a digital competitor? Think again. It is not the individual company that is most threatening. It is the ecosystem it forges.

In the digital age, competitive advantage goes to those who build an ecosystem, or network, that leverages digital technology for the benefit of the consumer and paves the way to multiple streams of revenue.

The concept of an ecosystem is of course not new. Apple famously pulled ahead of other mobile phones in its early days largely because it cultivated an ecosystem of software developers who created iPhone apps to meet every consumer niche and need. In the PC era, Intel had an alliance with Microsoft and cultivated an ecosystem of peripherals manufacturers that used Intel chips. Ensuring that their technologies worked together helped all of the players grow. Currently Microsoft uses an ecosystem of several thousand partners that install its products and services for enterprise customers, building its customer base while allowing Microsoft to focus on creating the software.

What's different among the digital giants is that their ecosystems are not just linear—that is, aligned with a company's supply chain—they are exponential and multidimensional. These new-generation ecosystems encompass a vast range of partners across multiple sectors. Alibaba, for example, known mostly as an e-commerce giant, has ecosystem partners as diverse as Weibo (for social media), Lyft (ride sharing), and Cainiao (logistics). Its voice-activated device Tmall Genie uses voice commands to order things from Alibaba's Tmall site, similar to Amazon's Alexa. When the market for Tmall Genie slowed, Alibaba created Tmall Genie Auto, a smart speaker with similar capabilities for cars, and expanded its ecosystem accordingly. In 2019 Alibaba had partnerships with BMW, Volvo, Audi, Renault, and Honda to install Tmall Genie Auto in some of their cars.

Competitive advantage comes from widening your lens to conceive of how an ecosystem could deliver something superior for the customer, and bringing partners onto your platform to share data, cutting-edge capabilities, and maybe even financial resources to help the entire ecosystem grow. Some ecosystem partners are creating joint loyalty programs; others are collaborating on innovation. Honeywell and Bigfinite, for example, are combining their strengths in process automation and controls (Honeywell) and data analytics, AI, and machine learning (Bigfinite) to help the pharmaceutical industry get drugs to the market faster.

Shared Growth and Benefits

Digital competitors often combine pieces from disparate industries to create a better, more complete experience for the consumer, or to lower costs, and therefore price, by eliminating intermediaries. The most powerful ecosystems go even further. A well-conceived ecosystem creates a network effect by which all participants—customers, partners, and the company itself—benefit and, together, drive exponential revenue growth.

In April 2019 CEO Jeff Bezos began his highly anticipated annual letter to Amazon shareowners with a column of numbers. Not profits or stock price, as you might expect. The numbers showed the growing percentage of Amazon's sales that came from independent third-party sellers on Amazon Marketplace over the previous twenty years. In 1999, the number was just 3 percent. By 2018, it was 58 percent, so more than half its total. This set of third-party sellers is part of the ecosystem that has helped drive Amazon's explosive growth.

Amazon helps its third-party sellers succeed by offering them a series of sophisticated tools the company developed to help them manage inventory and process payments. The sellers can use Amazon's fulfillment services to deliver their products faster and across a far broader geographic footprint than they otherwise could, as well as apply for loans from Amazon Lending. Merely listing an item on Amazon makes it discoverable by many more people. Roughly 54 percent of online consumers start their product search on Amazon's website—a higher percentage than those who start with Google.

As Amazon's eco-partners grow, so does Amazon. Cash increases, and the company accumulates increasingly more data. In Amazon's algorithm-driven world, data leads to better recommendations for the consumer, better insights into how to improve the consumer experience, and better management decisions. The consumer wins, too, by having more choices, lower prices, and more precise recommendations.

Amazon has been able to convert the massive amount of data flowing through its platform into multiple streams of revenue. It expanded from books to virtually every type of product—toys, pet supplies, consumer electronics, luggage, clothing, and jewelry—on its e-commerce site. Then there's the revenue from its Marketplace, from loans to third-party sellers, and from advertising that can be sharply targeted. Those successes have spawned entirely new offerings, from AWS to the Alexa virtual assistant, each of which now has an ecosystem and revenue streams of its own. As reported in the *Financial Times* in February 2020, Goldman Sachs may become part of Amazon's ecosystem. *FT*'s Laura Noonan wrote, "Goldman Sachs has begun building technology to facilitate the offering of loans to small and medium-sized businesses over Amazon's lending platform."

In today's world, it is virtually impossible to conceptualize a winning offer to a large number of customers without taking the ecosystem into account. Leaders of legacy companies must grasp the scale and scope of the ecosystems that have begun to emerge and, despite the complexity of so many moving parts, reimagine their own. The ecosystem has to be focused on the individual consumer's needs, get funded and be able to generate cash at the right pace, and lead to multiple streams of revenue, which will expand the ecosystem or become the seed of a new one. This imperative applies to business-to-business companies, not just consumer companies.

The Threat to Auto Ecosystems

For decades, auto manufacturers thought of their ecosystems as made up of independent entities in a linear sequence—the parts makers or vendors at the back end and the dealerships at the front. Senior leadership was riveted to their market shares: Ford versus GM, Toyota, and BMW. But today, a confluence of external forces has erased the industry boundaries, making automakers reconceptualize how they compete and with whom.

Tesla's founder, Elon Musk, did not invent electric cars, but he tapped into advances in battery technology and environmental concerns as he pushed to make electric vehicles a practical alternative to the internal combustion engine. Tesla began selling electric cars in 2008 and has boosted sales with new models introduced in the years that followed. Tesla got noticed not only because of Musk's bigger-than-life personality but also because the company's stylish high-quality electric cars were gaining converts.

Musk was unfazed when the makers of internal combustion engines, such as Mitsubishi and Peugeot and later Nissan, GM, and others, took their own plans for electric cars off the back burner. In a 2014 blog, he announced that "in the spirit of the open source movement," Tesla would open up its patents "for the advancement of electric vehicle technology." Tesla's technology was up for grabs.

Meanwhile, developments in cameras, sensors, processing capability, remote sensing, and artificial intelligence were bringing self-driving cars into the realm of reality. Driver assist technology made by Mobileye, founded in Israel in 1999, evolved into full-blown self-driving technology. In 2017, Intel bought the company.

Google started a self-driving car initiative in 2009, which it later named Waymo and spun off. And the Silicon Valley start-up Cruise Automation that was exploring self-driving technology caught the attention of GM, which acquired it in 2016.

The algorithms that handle the driving in autonomous vehicles (AVs) have to be trained, using lots of data from real cars on the road. Waymo and Tesla already had many years' worth of data when other companies began road testing their AVs in earnest in Pittsburgh, San Francisco, parts of Shanghai, and the outskirts of Beijing. In summer 2019, UPS was already using driverless trucks made by TuSimple for limited routes in Arizona.

Yet another set of disruptors collided with the automakers and tech companies in the last decade: ride-hailing start-ups like Uber and Lyft in the United States and Didi Chuxing in China. The famous line from professor and marketing guru Ted Levitt in 1969—that nobody really wanted a quarter-inch drill, they wanted a quarter-inch hole—became newly relevant. People didn't necessarily want to own a vehicle; they simply wanted to get from one place to another. The ride-hailers met that need with algorithmic platforms that matched people who needed to go somewhere with drivers who were willing to take them there. The availability of this convenient, lower-cost alternative called into question the whole premise of car ownership.

The ride-hailers got interested in AVs and began imagining a fleet of cars that were always available—operated by technology without human beings, who needed periodic breaks. The automakers became interested in transforming their products into a ride-sharing service and using AV technology, and technology companies sought ways to leverage their innovations.

Those unstoppable trends drove the auto manufacturing, ride-hailing, and tech sectors to gradually become part of the same competitive landscape. The following diagram shows the complexity of the mobility ecosystem:

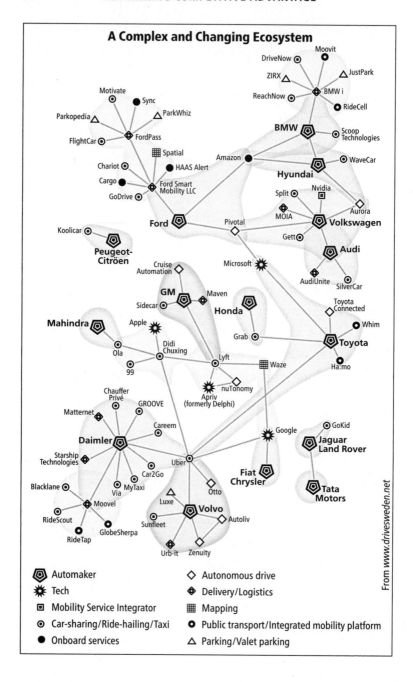

A Complex and Changing Ecosystem

From www.drivesweden.net

The ecosystems of automakers, tech companies, and ride-sharing and meal delivery businesses have been permanently scrambled. Even the finance companies like Soft-Bank's Vision Fund are part of the ecosystem's competitive edge, providing the cash required to develop new technologies. SoftBank owns Arm, a British semiconductor maker, and a stake in Nvidia, another chip maker.

Each of the major automakers has had to radically reconfigure its ecosystem to include a wider range of players and new kinds of relationships. As a rule of thumb, I believe every major player will need at least ten ecosystem partners to succeed. The choices they make today will determine the viability of their "mobility ecosystem" in years to come. Automakers know that demand for their core products is in secular decline and that building the right alliances for the future requires hard cash. They are forced to generate cash by selling assets. GM sold its European brand Opel and Vauxhall in 2017 and announced its exit from Australia, New Zealand, and Thailand in February 2020. Ford shifted its India operations to a joint venture with Mahindra and Mahindra, which will own 51 percent. All the automakers are narrowing their product lines and cutting jobs. They have to make fate-altering decisions very soon in the face of uncertainties about relationships and risks and rewards to come.

Emerging Mobility Ecosystems

Partnerships in the auto industry are not unheard of. Automakers have worked together on engine development, for example. But pooling intellectual capital and resources among longtime competitors is a huge change in mindset. A headline on Bloomberg.com on December 20, 2018, touches on this point: "BMW, Mercedes Pivot from Enemies to Partners in New Auto Era."

The German luxury carmakers had been bitter rivals for decades. But in 2015, they recognized that the digital era favored commonality and speed. Rather than developing their own individual mapping systems, and in an effort to set the standard for other car manufacturers, Daimler, BMW, and Audi jointly purchased a majority stake in Nokia's mapping business, Here. By late 2018, with technology in automobiles becoming even more sophisticated and pervasive, they were willing to take that collaboration even further, to include development of vehicle platforms, electric-car batteries, and autonomous-driving technology.

The German carmakers' pursuit of autonomous driving puts their nascent ecosystem in competition with a surprising mix of players, who are sorting themselves into ecosystems of their own.

In mid-2017, Lyft started building an ecosystem around an open-source software platform it launched. It forged partnerships with several technology suppliers in the self-driving space, including Waymo.

Lyft's Chinese counterpart, Didi Chuxing, which commanded 97 percent of the ride-sharing market in China after buying out Uber's Chinese operations in 2016, had been testing self-driving software made by Chinese automaker Qoros.

And yet another ecosystem was forming in China, orchestrated by Baidu, China's largest Internet company. Sometimes referred to as the Google of China because of its founding as an Internet search company, the tech giant has been pushing to be a leader in artificial intelligence. Why not apply AI to self-driving cars?

In 2017 Baidu had some catching up to do, but it had a plan. It launched a platform of data, applications, and software code, called Apollo, that partners could freely use to develop products for the autonomous vehicle market. It was an open-system approach, similar to what Google had used to scale up Android.

Creating a platform at the center of its ecosystem allowed the company to overcome a major drawback of being a latecomer: the lack of data. Within fourteen months, Baidu had drawn one hundred partners into its ecosystem, including Microsoft, Intel, Daimler, Chinese automaker BAIC, and parts suppliers. It amassed data from across its ecosystem and put the dataset on the Apollo platform.

Didi continues to compete fiercely against Baidu with a different ecosystem that now includes thirty-one automakers and parts suppliers. Its data comes largely from its ride-sharing vehicles across the globe. And it has formed joint ventures with Volkswagen and BAIC, a Chinese automaker, to manage its fleet and develop vehicles specifically for ride-sharing purposes.

But U.S. automakers are not sitting still. When GM pulled Cruise into its ecosystem by buying it outright, it set it up as an independent unit so as not to quash it. Then in October 2018 it brought cash funders into its ecosystem, partnering with Honda and SoftBank, both of which received equity stakes in Cruise in exchange for investing $2.75 billion and $2.25 billion, respectively.

The complexity and speed of the moving parts in an ecosystem can be overwhelming; shaping and reshaping the ecosystem should be one of your company's central leadership activities.

Keep your eye on your competitors' ecosystems, as well as your own. What players do they include, how are the ecosystems changing and adapting, how are they working to serve consumers better? And which eco-partners have been left out?

Ecosystems That Expand Capabilities and Revenue Growth

A properly reshaped ecosystem can lead to new opportunities and new business models. That was the case for UST, a California-based technology services company that has over a billion dollars in annual revenues and is growing at 24 percent a year. In its effort to meet the changing needs of its customers amid major shifts in technology, UST developed three kinds of partners in its ecosystem.

For most of the time since its founding in 1999, UST provided IT outsourcing services. Starting as a fourteen-member shop in India, it grew quickly as it developed a reputation among clients for reliable service and an unmatched ability to execute. By 2015, it was doing some $700 million in business a year, providing wide-ranging technology solutions to some large blue-chip customers, including top retailers, healthcare players, and financial institutions around the world.

While the business was strong, new kinds of technology were taking hold. Companies were desperately seeking help designing digital platforms that could be used to improve the quality and speed of decision-making and create better customer and employee experiences.

UST didn't believe in building the digital platforms all by itself. The executive team thought that would be too slow, and a large enterprise like UST might not be able to match the agility of a start-up. So the team conceived of a way to solve the problem by building an ecosystem to fill the gap. The ecosystem would also be a way to build out more innovative experiences, nimble infrastructure, and cost-effective, outcome-based solutions for clients.

Around 2015 the team began to search for start-up companies they could invest in that could bring new digital and algorithmic expertise and innovative applications to supplement UST's skills. They identified fifteen small companies that could help build digital platforms that would augment the tools and platforms UST itself was building. In some cases, UST bought a stake in the start-up; in others, they acquired the company outright. Some remained independent—they continued to market themselves while UST was able to present them to clients as well.

Apart from those investments and acquisitions, UST harnessed the innovative culture and entrepreneurial mindset within the company to incubate a number of digital platforms that became highly successful in the market. It also partnered with top academic institutions such as

MIT, Stanford, and the University of Pennsylvania to bring cutting-edge research to clients and make it relevant to clients' problems.

This ecosystem of platform builders allowed UST to meet its clients' changing needs while bringing new business to the start-ups. The small software companies also got the benefit of learning from each other, and most saw their market value increase.

As the leaders at UST assembled a critical mass of sought-after technology skills while maintaining their reputation for excellence, they saw an opportunity to take their platform design capability to Fortune 500 and Global 1000 customers. A few of those companies were already in their client base, but reaching others would be slow and expensive.

They decided that they needed another set of ecosystem partners that already had access to many of those companies. Part of UST's plan was to create platforms in which 80 percent of the design could be used by multiple companies in an industry or sector. Partnering with software companies that had complementary products or services and also had access to the biggest corporate clients would strengthen revenues and market share for everyone. Big corporate clients would get a more complete offering, and UST's ecosystem partners would be able to leverage UST's reputation to establish new relationships with corporate titans. Everyone would grow. By 2019, some of those ecosystem relationships had begun to mature.

Then ideas about another facet of the ecosystem began to bubble up. Dominant "big tech" companies have large enterprise clients, and these digital companies are constantly looking at developing new enterprise digital platforms to address these clients. UST, with its deep understanding of its customers' domains and business problems, is a natural ally to these digital companies. They now jointly offer digital systems that solve clients' needs at a fraction of the cost and time compared to what clients might spend building the tools and systems on their own.

Thinking in terms of ecosystems allowed UST to expand its capabilities efficiently and grow faster than they otherwise could. The ecosystem is continuously refreshed and ever-expanding for the latest technologies and cutting-edge innovations. And a multiplier effect kicked in as each of the three-hundred-plus smaller ecosystem partners grows its own capability and client base, giving UST more to offer its customers.

Legacy companies that try to compete on their own will be forced to compete against ecosystems like UST's on various fronts, such as lower and declining prices. By attempting to go it alone, they're less likely to find opportunities that create additional sources of revenue, and their market value will tend to decline.

How Funders Shape Ecosystems and Competitive Advantage

Most of the sprawling ecosystems that are emerging have been driven by business leaders, such as Amazon's Jeff Bezos, Alibaba's Jack Ma, or Baidu's Robin Li. But a few capital funders are playing a crucial role in shaping the competitive landscape by connecting the pieces.

In 2017, Masayoshi Son, the head of SoftBank Group, a massive Tokyo-based holding company he founded, saw the opportunity to give promising start-ups in the late stages of development larger sums of money to get them to so-called unicorn status (a billion dollars in market value) sooner. He had done it before, most notably turning his initial investment of $20 million in Alibaba into more than $5 billion at the time the company went public in 2014. He created SoftBank Vision Fund and rounded up a whopping $100 billion from the likes of Saudi Arabian sovereign wealth and hedge funds.

Vision Fund's large size had people wondering whether all that money could be deployed effectively, and how. That turned out not to be a problem. By 2019, the fund had invested all of the $100 billion across a range of companies including Uber, Arm Holdings, WeWork, Flipkart, and GM Cruise, and Masa Son had begun talking about raising another round of investment capital. (He did have an enormous loss in his investment in WeWork in 2019, which caused significant embarrassment and raised doubts about the viability of a new fund.)

But Masa Son is not just a large-scale passive investor. He is an architect of large-scale ecosystems. His stake in a company includes the intention to influence it, make connections between it and other similar companies, sometimes to combine it with another company. In pursuit of his vision, he alters the competitive advantage of other companies.

SoftBank's moves in the area of mobility demonstrate a broad and farsighted view of how the pieces can come together in ways that create greater value sooner.

Moving forward requires seamless connections among multiple systems and technology platforms, taking advantage of the latest technical developments, meeting a range of consumer preferences, and processing massive amounts of data to improve the outcomes of things like autonomous driving. Masa Son seems to be assembling the pieces of an extensive mobility ecosystem that can meet these requirements. As reported by Reuters in April 2019, SoftBank has placed "a $60 billion bet in more than 40 companies in a bid to steer the $3 trillion global automotive industry."

In 2014 SoftBank, along with Alibaba, took a stake in the Chinese ride-hailing company that is now Didi Chuxing. It also has stakes in Uber, Ola (Latin America's version), and Grab (Singapore's version). Partnerships with other players, including automakers Toyota, Honda, and GM, and a $2.5 billion investment, along with Honda's commitment of $2.75 billion, in GM Cruise reveal an even higher aim.

These investments are not intended to act as stand-alone companies but rather to help each other. A joint venture between SoftBank and Toyota called Monet Technologies (Monet is short for Mobility Network) will allow Toyota's digital platform for connected vehicles to coordinate with SoftBank's Internet of Things (IoT) platform. That way, Toyota can tap into more extensive sources of data and use it to eventually improve things like dispatching delivery services.

Standardization, coordination, and sharing among the various players are expected to speed the development of key technologies as well as their deployment. The diversity of players will allow for a broad range of solutions customized to commercial and individual needs, and flexibility in responding to regulations, whether by national or state (think California) governments. Whether Masayoshi Son succeeds or not (his execution has been falling short), he is influencing, and in some cases determining, the pattern of competition in these industries, including the shape of the ecosystems.

Apple's Emerging Healthcare Ecosystem

Apple is known for building an ecosystem of music producers around the iPod and an ecosystem of app developers around the iPhone. So you might expect it to create another ecosystem around its Apple Watch. What you might not realize is just how expansive that ecosystem is likely to be and how focused Apple seems to be on creating it.

Apple is now shaping it as its biggest, most complex ecosystem yet, leveraging what it has done well before: focus intensely on the consumer, protect consumer privacy, figure out how to make money and build incentives, and connect hardware and software. The central idea underlying Apple's ecosystem is to pull data from all sources, including the customer or patient, into its machine learning engine, to process it and feed it back to the relevant suppliers of data in order to improve the quality and cost of healthcare.

Healthcare broadly defined is a huge market, representing some 20 percent of U.S. GDP, or about $13 trillion and growing at around 6 percent a year. It includes a broad mix of players, from physicians and hospitals to insurers, medical research institutions, and medical device makers. Some players are big, some are small. Some are more digitally advanced than others. Their business models vary greatly, as do the regulations they must adhere to.

What causes the greatest frustration and the gravest danger to patients are the information disconnects between the various entities. Data is dispersed, and systems are incompatible. Those disconnects create a lot of waste and excess cost, leaving plenty of room for fraud to go undetected. Worse, miscommunication can cause overtreatment, errors, or delays in diagnosis that directly affect a patient's health.

Apple's answer is to build an ecosystem focused on a customized end-to-end experience of healthcare that will once and for all overcome the disconnects and create a single source of truth. Ambitious, yes, but as CEO Tim Cook told Jim Cramer of CNBC's *Mad Money,* "If you zoom out into the future, and you look back, and you ask the question, 'What was Apple's greatest contribution to mankind?' It will be about health."

It makes sense that Apple would tackle this area, given its relentless focus on the consumer, its mastery of integrating hardware and software, and its experience in building ecosystems. It also has long had a penchant for protecting consumer privacy, which will help it gain trust around protecting patient information. And it has a global army of app developers, and a base of 900 million users worldwide (you're never far from an iPhone charger in airports and limousines).

Apple's conceptualization of a healthcare ecosystem is squarely focused on the individual consumer. Everything revolves around the individual, and data about his or her health remains under his or her control. Apple provides the means for health records to be consolidated in one place and format, and the necessary safeguards as data flows to and from the patient and caregivers. It also aggregates and encrypts it for use in medical research.

Standardizing data will eliminate a lot of the waste in record keeping alone and, combined with algorithms, can detect fraudulent billing. It ensures that data from various medical practices and health centers can be used by others, so records don't get lost when patients change doctors or hospitals, and doctors get a fuller view of a patient's medical history.

Access to more data allows researchers to analyze it in a zillion ways for testing purposes, as well as to screen candidates for drug trials. Research and development of drugs and medical devices can be made faster and better (Amgen has already cut its development cycle by five years, so dramatic improvements are possible).

Data also brings regulation into the twenty-first century, providing stronger evidence of a drug or procedure's effectiveness.

Healthcare is also on the radar of digital giants Amazon and Alphabet, as well as consumer electronics makers like Samsung and Garmin. It remains to be seen whether

Apple's consumer-focused healthcare ecosystem will set the standard or become part of an alliance with other players. It would be wrong, though, to think of Apple as being overly optimistic or futuristic. Its construction of an expansive healthcare ecosystem is already under way.

In 2013 and 2014, Apple hired numerous people with expertise in medical devices, sensor technology, and fitness. Divya Nag, a twenty-three-year-old who had dropped out of Stanford to cofound Stem Cell Theranostics, was recruited to Apple's Special Projects Group. Nag later described that work as "essentially to push boundaries and dream of what the future of health care looks like and what role Apple can play."

In June 2014 Apple introduced a feature on the iPhone called Health, which collects basic health and fitness information, like how many steps an individual took that day. Then came HealthKit, a software platform that takes data from multiple sources, makes it compatible, and allows independent developers to create apps that tap into that data.

Apple followed up with ResearchKit, another set of tools for app developers, this one aimed at facilitating medical research. In 2016, 23andMe, the gene testing company, integrated its data with ResearchKit, allowing researchers to use genetic information as well.

Much of the data about an individual's health comes from caregivers and labs, but it also gets picked up in real time through so-called wearable devices. That's where the Apple Watch plays a pivotal role in the ecosystem. It generates data directly from a person's body. Individuals can use that information to monitor their fitness, or they can allow it to be fed directly into algorithms that process it instantaneously. In December 2018, the FDA cleared two optional features of the Watch that use algorithms, one to detect irregular heart rhythms and another that combines an electrical sensor on the Series 4 Watch with an electrocardiogram app and algorithm. Both are intended to provide early warning signs of possible atrial fibrillation or other heart problems.

More surprising than the apps and the connectivity between physical devices and software is the quickening pace of partnerships that Apple is forging with insurers, researchers, and laboratories. It has launched studies with more than half a dozen leading research institutions, including Stanford Medicine and NYU Langone Medical Center, to tackle problems like sleep apnea, concussions, depression, and autism. Neurology professors Gregory Knauss and Nathan Crone, researchers at Johns Hopkins, used the Apple Watch to record data in a study of epileptic seizures.

Apple has partnered with health insurers Aetna and UnitedHealth, which use the Watch in programs to incentivize people to achieve fitness goals. Multiple reports suggest Apple is working on similar arrangements with Medicare plans.

Some twenty-five major hospital systems representing 14 percent of total hospital beds in the United States, as well as hundreds of other healthcare providers and laboratories, are hooked into Apple's electronic medical records system. In 2018 Apple opened a clinic, called AC Wellness Clinic, for employees, which is likely a testing ground for even more beneficial uses of consumer-centered data.

As is true for any robust ecosystem, Apple's creates a virtuous circle. Researchers get access to more granular data, providers get a timely feed of information about symptoms and compliance with treatment, and consumers have greater control of information from multiple sources. Bureaucracy is reduced throughout, reducing cost and risk. Everyone learns, spurring innovation and improvements in healthcare. Apple facilitates the collection and use of data and can use it to improve its own software and devices. As start-ups invent solutions for some part of an individual's life cycle, Apple can bring them into its ecosystem.

Any competitor to Apple, as well as hospital chains, labs, and pharmaceutical companies, should be looking at the bigger picture of the healthcare ecosystem that is developing and decide if they want to be a part of it or another one, or have the audacity to start their own. Some have begun. Hospitals such as Brigham and Women's Hospital in Boston and Mayo Clinic have begun to share identifiable patient data with IBM, Microsoft, and Amazon.

Managing Ecosystems

Managing an ecosystem requires a specific set of leadership skills. Few companies have people with exactly that experience on their résumés, and it's not a job category headhunters can readily search. Senior executives need to identify people who show an aptitude in designing metrics, resolving issues around sharing intellectual property, and negotiating contracts and exit clauses. At the end of the day, it's about building relationships with people from other cultures and with different incentives. In my view, the person in charge should report directly to the CEO, and he or she will have to build a team of people, essentially a whole department, to manage the ecosystem.

Ecosystems are never permanent. Because the world is moving at such a ferocious speed, technology change continues to accelerate, and consumer expectations continually evolve, finding new partnerships and exiting old ones has to become routine. Existing relationships have to be nurtured, as well, because successful eco-partners are likely to be approached by other companies and ecosystems. Keeping the ecosystem in balance in terms of data and moneymaking is an ongoing challenge as profit pools shift.

But the predominate challenge is to conceive of the ecosystem in its entirety, how it will deliver a great experience for the consumer, how the partners will enhance each other's capabilities, and how success will be measured and shared.

Not everyone has the cognitive ability to conceptualize business platforms on a grand scale. Not everyone will have the imagination to think that big or the confidence to pull other companies into their orbit.

One thing that can help is knowledge about algorithms. You don't have to be a technology wizard—Jack Ma, founder of Alibaba, was not. And you might start with a simpler version of an ecosystem, as Amazon did when it sold only books online.

If you make the effort to learn about algorithms, you will come to appreciate how they can overcome previous obstacles, such as customizing products on a very large scale. A basic working knowledge of digital technology can alter leaders' imagination, expand their scope, and at the same time build their courage and resolve, all of which are essential to being the architect of a powerful ecosystem in the digital age.

Now you are familiar with several of the building blocks of creating competitive advantage in the digital age. As always, businesses must also create value for shareholders. Otherwise people at all organizational levels will suffer the consequences of a downward spiral. The next chapter explains how digital companies create new models for making money in ways that power their growth and allow them to serve customers and shareholders better at the same time.

CHAPTER 6

MONEYMAKING FOR DIGITALS

Rule #4: Moneymaking is geared for huge cash generation, not earnings per share, and the new law of *increasing* returns. Funders understand the difference.

Born-digital companies can consume a ton of cash in
their early years in their high-speed race for customers, revenue growth, content, and reach. Their earnings per share—
the stock market's favorite metric—can be zero or deeply
negative for years, if not decades. Yet these companies seem
to have the capital they need, because some investors know
what the leaders of digital companies know: that moneymaking is different in the digital age. Of course the components of moneymaking—things like revenues, cash, gross
margin, cost structure, and funding—are the same as ever.
But the emphasis, the patterns, the timing, and the relationships among them are different. Using these differences to
create value for both the consumer and shareholders *at the*

same time is a new kind of business savvy and a source of competitive advantage.

When Amazon first started selling books online, its cash needs were relatively small, because customers paid for books immediately, while Amazon did not have to pay the publisher for several months. Its need for cash exploded when it reached the point where it needed to build scale to grab the additional myriad retail opportunities that were within easy reach.

For many digital companies, especially those that are building two-sided platforms, the need for large amounts of cash comes very early on. Two-sided businesses such as Airbnb and Uber, for example, have to get a large number of users on both the demand side and the supply side—those wanting a ride and those providing a ride—in order to create value for consumers.

Today's digital giants exist because funders have been willing to provide huge sums of cash for extended periods of time, and to sometimes team up with other funders to provide even more. When Japan's SoftBank launched its $100 billion Vision Fund in 2016 to help start-ups grow on a large scale, skeptics doubted that SoftBank CEO Masayoshi Son could raise that much money, let alone find enough opportunities to invest it. But he did, receiving billions of dollars from Saudi Arabia's sovereign wealth fund, Abu Dhabi's Mubadala Investment Co., and others to add to SoftBank's own investment of $28 billion.

Vision Fund invested in eighty-eight digital companies. The plan was to fund the start-ups' fast growth, then take them public to reap a return on the value their fast growth would have created. SoftBank's pre–Vision Fund investment in Alibaba, as I mentioned in an earlier chapter, had grown by billions of dollars, and Vision Fund earned a 60 percent return when it sold its stake in Flipkart to Walmart. But in 2019, the market soured on initial public offerings of companies that gobbled cash. Following Uber's IPO, for example, the stock went into free fall and settled at about two-thirds of its IPO value, putting a major dent in the value of Vision Fund's stake. Slack's share price fell hard after its IPO a few months later. WeWork had to postpone its IPO and needed a $9.5 billion infusion from SoftBank to remain afloat.

While market valuations have come down to earth, and not every investment has a big payoff, promising digital companies continue to attract funding. Tiger Fund, Tencent, Sequoia, and others continue to search for companies that need cash and have the ability to scale up.

Every company should understand how digital technology changes the basics of moneymaking. They should know that funding flows easily to some businesses precisely because their moneymaking models exploit these differences. Digital companies can prosper, for example, by offering a lower price *and* a customized experience. Investment firms are willing to back these companies as they race to grab the next opportunity that will amplify their advantage. Aggressive financial backing lets some start-ups and even digital giants forge ahead at a pace that their unfunded competitors cannot match. The combination of a robust digital moneymaking model and a bold source of funding is tough to beat. Those businesses that do not get such backers are at a competitive disadvantage and are highly vulnerable to others who may permanently change the competitive order.

Cash Gross Margin

Through Amazon's early life, outsiders wondered how long investors would wait for the company to make a profit and, later, why its stock was so overvalued. Rounds of short sellers frequently renewed their conviction that shareholders were about to exit the stock en masse. I remember a conversation I had in 2013 with the CEO of a large corporation, who noted Amazon's negative earnings the previous year and assured me that "the chickens will come home to roost." But Jeff Bezos continued to run the business as he had from the start, with a laser focus on continuously improving the customer experience, centered on a digital platform, using an ever-expanding ecosystem, and building its customer base.

Bezos's business acumen was to focus not on earnings per share, Wall Street's favorite metric, but on revenue growth and cash gross margin. Amazon has in fact been accumulating copious amounts of cash.

In the digital era, it is possible to give the consumer something better, and at a lower price, because a digital platform makes the cost of delivering an additional unit incrementally low. The cost of a new Netflix subscriber viewing a series the company has already produced, or Amazon allowing third parties to sell their products on the e-commerce site it has already built, is close to zero.

As the cost of each additional unit shrinks, the benefit is passed to customers, increasing the chances of keeping those customers and attracting new ones. Revenues grow, as does something less obvious: gross margin.

Gross margin—revenue minus the direct costs of those goods—is often expressed as a percentage. For example, in 2002, the first year Amazon reported a profit, its gross margin was 25 percent. For 2018, its gross margin was 40 percent.

Now consider how much cash those numbers can represent. In 2002, Amazon's revenues were $3.93 billion; 25 percent of that amount was $983 million. By 2018, revenues had ballooned to $232 billion; 40 percent of that amount is a whopping $93 billion. This is cash it can allocate for growth or dividends.

This is where the power of the *law of increasing returns,* which I explained briefly in chapter 4, is on full display. As digital companies grow revenues and improve percentage gross margin, they exponentially increase their gross margin in cash. In essence they become a cash-generation machine. The S curve takes a sharp upward turn, like this:

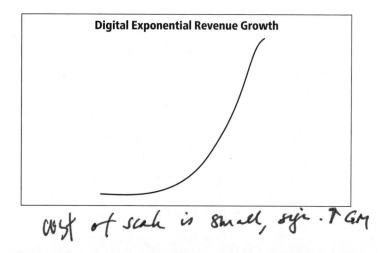

cost of scale is small, syn . ↑ GM

The gross margins of born-digital companies are generally higher than those of their conventional counterparts. While Amazon's gross margin in 2018 was 40 percent, Walmart's gross margin was around 25 percent. Despite negative earnings at Netflix, its gross margin has been healthy.

Higher gross margins are partly a function of being a digital company, but savvy leaders manage gross margins to widen the advantage.

Gross margin is like an MRI of the company's money-making model. It shows whether the pricing, direct costs, repeat usage, discounts, and mix of services, customers, and ecosystem partners is a healthy combination. Jeff Bezos has said many times that he always keeps his eye on cash gross margin. Steve Jobs did, too. Apple's gross margin is about 39 percent—the highest of all computer and cell-phone manufacturers in the world. Born-digital leaders know that once they have a healthy gross margin, if they are able to scale up, the payoff will be huge.

Leaders ask, Will a high volume of customers pay this price to produce the desired gross margin? If not, how can we get more revenues, introduce new services, change the mix we offer, or invest more cash to grow revenue in a way that boosts gross margin? Uber's gross margin is 50 percent. If it can get to 60 percent, it can use the additional cash gross margin to attract and retain drivers, and the company will be fine. If its gross margin slips, it might falter. But going to 60 percent gross margin requires innovation and cost reductions in an intensive competitive marketplace.

Analyzing cash gross margin is not actually a numbers

game. It is a matter of using data and analytic tools to understand the elements that are producing cash gross margin and to perhaps make some decisions to change it. Which movies should we produce for which subscribers, and at what cost? Reed Hastings has data and algorithms to help his team answer that, but decision makers also use their intuition about which elements to change. Which business should we go into next? Jeff Bezos can crowdsource and analyze the answer as he did when he first went into books, but the decision is partly intuitive.

Use of Cash

Digital giants also reflect their business savvy in their intense focus on how they use cash—where to invest it, how much, and how soon. The sums of cash they are willing to spend can be a very high percentage of their revenue and cash gross margin. Even when they generate a lot of cash, they often turn to outside sources for additional funding.

While Wall Street continues to use earnings per share as a dominant measure of a company's worth, digital giants refuse to let the ups and downs of EPS dissuade them from funding growth. Expansive growth is as deeply ingrained in most digital leaders as incremental improvement in EPS is in traditional companies.

In the digital world, a meager or delayed investment is a competitive disadvantage. Many legacy companies find themselves in that difficult spot. As they try to fund a new S curve, they get caught in a liquidity trap; they need cash from their core business and therefore cannot neglect it. Many are facing declines in volume and in revenue and cash gross margin because of pricing pressure on their company or the industry overall. They have to cut prices to stay competitive and may try to compensate for shrinking margins by acquiring a competitor. Despite management's good intentions to build the future, the core business tends to get the cash.

This is where bold thinking about cash allocation becomes highly controversial, and critical to the company's future. How can they sustain their core business *and* get a digital business off the ground? People's fears and frustrations come out when these topics get discussed in the executive suite. I have been privy to many such conversations. The leader of a company's core business spoke with raw emotion and worry when he put it this way: "My unit produces all this cash, and you want to put it into a very uncertain venture that will consume cash at an increasing rate. I need that cash to prevent my revenues from declining. We will lose on both ends."

Some companies manage the liquidity trap by creating a separate company and getting outsiders to fund it. Others decide to exit the core business altogether and use the cash they extracted to fund an entirely new venture.

Delphi, the world's third-largest supplier to auto manufacturers, divided itself into two companies in 2017, to sharpen the focus on technology development and allow for differences in the use of cash and the ability to attract capital. Delphi Technologies focused on power train development, and Aptiv focused on technology for autonomous vehicles. Glen De Vos, Delphi senior vice president and chief technology officer, said at the time: "There are suddenly becoming two different types of investors. The people that really are going to be focused on the powertrain investments, we're seeing them veer away from the investors that are really focused on more of the tech. We're at a great point right now where we've had two very healthy businesses with great outlooks, but at some point, they're going to start coming in conflict with each other in terms of resource consumption, capital investment and those types of things."

When a born-digital company reaches the point at which cash generation turns positive, it can use that cash to fund the next round of innovations for the consumer or build an entirely new S curve in what could be another very large market space. This pattern of allocating cash to new initiatives and reaping yet more cash is unmistakable at Google, Alibaba, Amazon, Adobe, and B2W. Provided that management focuses on the customer and is disciplined in how they innovate and execute, the company becomes a self-perpetuating cash-generation machine.

Amazon spends cash each time it expands into other areas of a consumer's life experience or into new regions. Its pattern is to fund multiple experiments, any one or more of which could be large scale. Those that continue to show promise get additional funding. Although there have been failures, which Bezos is quick to acknowledge, the successes generate the enormous cash that allows for even more experiments, with potentially additional big payoffs. Amazon's cash generation continues to increase, from some $60 billion gross margin cash generation in 2017 to a projected

$160 billion by 2021, enough to fund its own chipmaking division or quantum computers or some other potential big-ticket initiatives.

As aggressive as their pursuit of growth can be, digital giants are quick to pull out of unprofitable areas and to reallocate cash to something that has more promise. Fast change is second nature for them. Their intense focus on the consumer and early testing of new ideas prevents them from wasting resources on something customers will not pay for. Or to state it more positively, they spend their money on what the customer cares about. They use data to experiment, test, and analyze before they place their bets.

A Digital Company's Capex Is Opex

Costs are different for a digital company in the early going. Money is spent to acquire customers through marketing and promotions, to hire software engineers to build and maintain their digital platform, and for collecting data and developing the ecosystem. There is a stark contrast between born-digital companies and traditional companies in two areas: operating expenses and G&A (general and administrative) costs.

Most companies have capital expenditures of some kind, along with a robust and long-established process to evaluate them. Metrics like IRR (internal rate of return) and ROI (return on investment) are commonly used to approve or reject investments that have a long time horizon in terms of money committed to them and the payoff.

For a digital company, capex looks like opex. Much of the foundation for the business is not a hard asset, like a building or manufacturing equipment, that requires capital expenditures (capex). The cost of building the future takes the form of compensation paid to software developers and other technology experts, licenses for external software and services, and marketing efforts to build scale. Spending on those things gets recorded on the profit and loss statement as operating expenses (opex) in the here and now. Listed on a financial statement according to generally accepted accounting principles, those operating costs reduce current earnings. Earnings per share (EPS) takes a hit. But because opex is tax deductible and you therefore pay less in taxes, it increases cash in the till.

Negative EPS scares some business people away, but leaders of digital companies do not let it curb their appetite for growth. After years of steadily rising profits, Amazon wasn't shy in 2019 about signaling that its growth spurt has not ended. A headline in *The New York Times* made exactly that point: "Amazon's Profit Falls as Company Buys Growth." It was hastening its move toward using its own delivery service. Sorting centers, distribution facilities, and hubs near airports cost money, to the tune of more than half of its cash gross margin, a sum Bezos was willing to spend in pursuit of even faster delivery for customers. If you were to reduce Amazon's growth rate to the level of a typical retailer, its opex would drop and the company would show great earnings per share.

The willingness of these digital companies to spend heavily should not be construed as a willingness to waste resources. Streamlining costs may be a low priority in the months and years of building a digital platform and achieving scale, but no digital company succeeds for long without using technology in ways that keep expenses low. Amazon is fiercely disciplined in containing costs and keeping bureaucracy to a minimum. Along with the efficiency of generating huge revenues from its digital platform and AWS, Amazon's use of algorithmic and robotic automation helps explain why its G&A cost is less than 2 percent of revenues.

Amazon's low G&A percentage is a useful benchmark for some, but the specific numbers and patterns vary with a company's moneymaking model. It remains to be seen how venturing into physical stores will affect Amazon's general and administrative costs and how beefing up its online share will bring Walmart's down.

Uber faces intense competition and depends heavily on people, so it spends a large portion of its revenues in two categories: sales and marketing (28 percent) and R&D (18 percent). As the company has become more competitive and grown faster in recent years, those percentages have come down. Revenues doubled from 2016 to 2017 and grew by 42 percent from 2017 to 2018. G&A shrank from 26 percent of revenues in 2016 to 13 percent in 2018.

Companies that are transitioning to be digital have to totally rejigger their cost structure. Most costs need to be subjected to algorithmic analysis to detect patterns and find anomalies. The increased use of data should drive productivity improvement day in, day out, which can boost cash gross margins and lower prices for the consumer. In banking, an expense ratio (total expenditures divided by revenue) of 52 percent is considered to be respectable. But the CEO of one bank that I am familiar with, on the verge of digitization, told his team that the expense ratio had to go down to 35 percent. His benchmark was the emerging field of fintech. His implication was that doing things the old way would not get them there. They couldn't hide behind government regulations and had to think radically about how to eliminate waste and improve decision-making with the help of data analytics. In my work around the globe, I am noticing companies setting cost-reduction goals of 30 percent or 50 percent.

Expenses are also lower at digital giants because they tend to have fewer organizational layers and less bureaucracy. After digitizing its business, Fidelity Wealth Management has been able to reorganize its associates into just three organizational layers, improving decision-making and speed without losing accountability (see chapter 7).

Revenues and Growth Trajectories

Digital companies are better equipped than their traditional counterparts to create a stream of *recurring revenues* from ongoing relationships with their existing customers. The digital connection makes it easier to keep customers engaged and generates more useful data. Algorithms can then help detect the causes of certain behaviors, including customer defections, and test ways to improve the customer experience.

Those efforts can reduce the churn rate (the proportion

of dropped customers versus new ones), which in turn reduces costs. Netflix spent three years developing an algorithm that reduced churn by analyzing the relevance of content and the demographics of customers who left and did not come back.

Selling a subscription, as Netflix, Adobe, and Amazon do, provides a more predictable stream of recurring revenues. A subscription is like an annuity for the company offering it, reducing cyclicality. It is a convenience and a savings for the customer. For Adobe customers, a subscription lets them use the software without a heavy up-front investment.

Still, revenues from subscriptions are only as reliable as the customer experience. Netflix may make good use of data and algorithms, but if it cannot convert its data into something customers really want, at the right price, customers might well switch to another streaming option.

Companies that offer new experiences to existing customers create *new streams of revenue,* and the cost of acquiring those customers is zero. New revenues might come from simply regrouping offerings.

What ultimately determines the company's viability over time is the ability to turn cash spending (which suppresses EPS) into future efficient revenue growth. In today's world, that means starting whole *new cash-generating trajectories,* not just extending existing ones. The shelf life of consumers' habits and expectations is extremely short, and the time horizon for competitive advantage has shrunk accordingly.

Digital giants do not see revenue growth as a single trajectory but as a series of S curves, each the result of good ideas they experiment with and test. If you have a product that is right for the market and it takes off, it can fund many other trajectories. Apple's iPad, iTunes, and iPhone didn't come at once. One helped fund the next. Success on a massive scale allows for massive resources to be channeled into something new. The success of Amazon's e-commerce allowed it many other experiments, some of which were noted failures but some of which have themselves become huge moneymakers.

Amazon created an entirely new S curve with AWS, its huge and highly profitable cloud services business. The basic technology existed for Amazon's own use, but learning how customers would want to use it and making it work for many different situations took several years. It took more than seven years to develop Amazon's Alexa, as it did for the Kindle before.

Moneymaking Models

A moneymaking model explains how the various components of making money work together. I use the term *moneymaking model* instead of *business model* because there are many interpretations of what a business model is, some of which are overcomplicated. Moneymaking keeps things simple and concrete. How do revenue growth, gross margin, and cash actually link?

Uber decided to go into many new cities quickly to establish its brand with the global traveling public. It sought to form alliances and collect data ahead of other players, even if it meant incurring big losses.

The direct costs of providing the ride-hailing service are the cost of the driver, cost to acquire customers, and maybe some direct labor. Uber also spends a lot on general and administrative costs, which probably include PR and regulatory work, and on R&D to develop self-driving cars.

For 2019, Uber had revenues of $14 billion. Gross margin was around 50 percent, about the same as it had been for a few years. Sales and marketing costs were 32 percent of revenues, general and administrative costs were 22 percent, and R&D was 34 percent. Assuming its cash allocation stays the same, it needs gobs of cash to acquire new customers, new drivers, and new offices for the new locations, and for financial incentives to recruit and retain the technology talent it needs to drive innovation. At a revenue growth rate of 38 percent a year, as Uber projected, in five years revenues could go to $70 billion.

Think of what the sources of that revenue growth might be: more trips per customer, new customers, and higher usage through better logistics and things like Uber Eats. Uber has about 111 million active platform users per month, with total trips of 7 billion a year. Each customer takes an average of 5.7 trips per month. What will it take to increase the number of trips and how will that increase gross margin, profitability, and cash?

Uber's moneymaking model could work. At the same time, passengers can choose Lyft or Didi Chuxing or another ride-share company in some places, so keeping customers could also become more costly. And driver costs could rise. If Uber cannot maintain its cash gross margin as it increases revenues, its moneymaking model might prove to be untenable. Hurt by the coronavirus shutdown, in April 2020 Uber withdrew financial guidance for the year and said it would take a $2 billion write-down.

Moneymaking models are always susceptible to change. The primary focus needs to always be on the consumer, but external factors also matter. Maintaining an advantage takes vigilance and a willingness to change. As we've seen, even Fortune 500 companies can disappear if they cannot adapt.

Legacy leaders may be determined to change their business, and boards might support the idea. But the legacy psychology tends to seep in. Are there guarantees that this initiative will work? How can the company put that much money on the line? How will we explain the drop in EPS to Wall Street?

Digitization should reduce costs over time and lessen the need for capital. But it will likely require a maniacal focus on the customer along with an entirely new moneymaking model, based on data and a digital platform, to produce higher revenue growth, gross margin, and cash. A declining S curve of the core business should be a sign of urgency. A decline in sports channel ESPN seemed to spur Disney CEO Bob Iger to take action.

Funding and Funders

By late October 2019, the video streaming wars were in full gear. Disney's control of Hulu had solidified, and its Disney+ streaming service was about to launch. Apple debuted its AppleTV+ streaming service, and WarnerMedia announced that its HBO Max streaming service would begin in May 2020. NBCUniversal teased that a streaming service called Peacock was coming. Meanwhile, Netflix CEO Reed Hastings was doubling down on his commitment to invest in content, even as licensing deals with the networks and studios became more expensive.

Analysts continued to speculate about where consumers would go, how much Netflix would be hurt by the loss of licensed material, and who would produce the best content and have the deepest pockets to fund it going forward.

In 2019, Netflix was the clear leader in terms of the number of subscribers, breadth of content, and intensity of customer engagement. But the company was chewing up a ton of cash to acquire customers globally, and it was cranking up its spending on new content—from $13 billion in 2018 to an estimated $17 billion for 2019. It was going on a spending spree to secure studio space in places such as Albuquerque, Surrey, Toronto, and New York.

In July 2019 the company said that they expected free cash flow to be negative by about $3.5 billion in 2019. And cash flow, they said, would continue to be negative for several years, albeit less so after 2020 as the member base, revenues, and operating margins grew. The timing of cash inflows and outflows would also change, Netflix noted, because creating original content requires paying production costs up front before the titles are released and revenues materialize. In April 2019, Netflix raised €1.2 billion and $900 million in high-yield bonds, while acknowledging that it might borrow more.

The future of the video streamers will depend in part on funding. Disney generates cash from other sources, such as theme parks and movie releases. To ease the financial pain of its Disney+ launch and fatten the subscription numbers, it struck a deal for Verizon to offer its customers one year free of Disney+. Verizon would pay Disney an undisclosed fee for each subscription, potentially 17 million of them.

Apple had $245 billion in cash on hand in 2019, and Amazon had $25 billion. Netflix funders will have to be convinced that if Netflix executes the right content, and has the right way to acquire customers and the right way to increase usage, it will become even bigger, and a huge cash generator, along the lines of Amazon, Google, Facebook, and Alibaba. As CEO Reed Hastings said at *The New York Times* DealBook Conference in November 2019, "Time will be the real competition. . . . How do consumers vote with their evenings?" The customer offering has to be right, and the moneymaking model has to be persuasive enough to interest funders.

The issue is *funders,* not just *funding.* There is benefit in securing money from investors and organizations who practice 10x or 100x thinking.

In 2017 Westfield Corp., run by its founder, Frank Lowy, and his sons, operated high-end shopping malls across the United States. Their response to the changes disrupting the retail landscape was to allow another real estate firm, Paris-based Unibail-Rodamco SE, to take over its malls. The agreement allowed the Lowys to keep control of one business unit that they would use as the seed for a separate company tailored to the digital age. Unibail would have a

10 percent stake in the spin-off. The deal freed the Lowys to focus on a concept they believed was ripe for the digital world: a digital platform that aimed to help retail clients analyze their own customer data and, by combining it with data from multiple sources, create a fuller picture of the consumer. The digital company, called OneMarket, was listed on the stock market in 2018. The platform launched in 2019 and acquired a number of well-known retailers as clients. But OneMarket was burning through a lot of cash, and when big client Nordstrom failed to renew its contract, the stock market turned cold. OneMarket tried—but failed—to find a buyer. Whether or not the customer offering was right, OneMarket's funders were clearly not convinced.

A funder's desire for large-scale investment and large-scale return, its willingness to extend the time frame, especially in the cash-guzzling phase, and, in some cases, active participation in shaping the ecosystem or market is a considerable competitive advantage. In private equity, for example, there is little concern today about EPS. The focus is on market share, growth, and valuations based mostly on factors other than earnings.

Chinese Internet giant Tencent has amassed stakes in 277 start-ups since 2013. In 2017 alone it bought stakes in more than eighty public companies for a total value of $33 billion. It chooses companies with leading technologies or research as well as top players in high-growth markets "where we can share our experience and contribute to building the Internet ecosystems."

A company that can convincingly explain how it will

meet a large consumer need, how its digital platform will work, how the ecosystem will be shaped, and how the moneymaking will work has a good shot at finding a deep-pocketed backer. A track record of accomplishment, even one that doesn't include positive EPS, can keep the money flowing, reducing the liquidity risk during the company's expansion.

Ever-increasing negative cash flows have begun to worry some funders and investors, but there's no sign yet that these investors are at their limit. Digital companies have earned unprecedented freedom with their moneymaking models, and they are likely to maintain that competitive advantage when it comes to growth and how to fund it.

We have now seen several building blocks of competitive advantage: creating a market space by innovating for the consumer, putting a digital platform at the center, building an ecosystem, and figuring out the moneymaking. Companies are not machines. Human energy brings these activities to life. In the digital age, people can work differently to make better, faster decisions and synchronize their work. The next chapter shows how, and illustrates the competitive advantage that derives from doing so.

CHAPTER 7

TEAMS INSTEAD OF ORGANIZATIONAL LAYERS

Rule #5: People, culture, and work design form a "social engine" that drives innovation and execution personalized for each customer.

One of the greatest and least recognized competitive advantages that today's digital giants have over traditional players is a powerful *social engine* that drives their exponential growth. This social engine—which includes the company's people, culture, and way of getting work done—has tremendous energy and speed. It eliminates bureaucracy and achieves what many companies find so elusive: the ability to continuously adapt and innovate on behalf of the consumer. Their social engines run with discipline while freeing up people's imagination. And they create value for customers, ecosystem partners, shareholders, and employees all at the same time.

Most digital companies operate with as few as three or four organizational layers. As big as Amazon is, it has just three organizational layers below the level of the top executive in some major parts of the business. The bulk of the work is accomplished by teams, each of which includes the critical expertise needed to take the project or assignment from initial concept to delivery or operations. Amazon's Jeff Wilke, CEO of Worldwide Consumer, refers to his company's mechanism for organizing work as "separable single-threaded teams." Members focus solely on the one thing their team is expected to deliver, and their daily work is shielded from any other company responsibilities.

Breaking work into bite-size missions and giving stand-alone teams the autonomy to figure out the "how" leads to faster, better decision-making. Coupled with agile methodologies borrowed from the world of software development and fast feedback enabled by a digital platform, teams can quickly test a prototype, or minimum viable product (MVP), and use data to revise and relaunch it very quickly. Cycle times for innovation get shorter, and risk is reduced.

The best digital companies recognize that structure goes only so far—and that success ultimately depends on the quality of its people. They select new hires and team leaders with as much attention to values and behavior as to their talent and skills. When Fidelity Personal Investing changed to a team-based structure as part of its digital transformation, President Kathy Murphy and her team took time to personally review hundreds of individuals in excruciating detail to find leaders who would help empower diverse teams to solve problems and create value (I'll say more on that later in the chapter). Team leaders who adhere to the principles of *simultaneous dialogue*, where everyone hears the same thing at the same time, and servant leadership, that is, helping others achieve a higher purpose, expand a team's collective learning and fire up people's imagination. They increase the chances of breakthroughs and big wins.

Technology plays a key role in giving people greater freedom to do their work. Algorithms automate many decisions and produce a slew of metrics that can help guide decision-making. Fidelity PI now has over a thousand metrics. Amazon has sixty-two pages' worth, and the search for better metrics continues.

Digital platforms make real-time information transparent to people in other parts of the organization, so teams can self-correct, requiring less need for human supervision. People feel liberated to spend more time doing what they inherently want to do, which is to contribute to something meaningful, and grow professionally. The original iPhone is the product of just this kind of approach at Apple, where a small team huddled for two years working on the secretive "Purple" project.

These components of a digital giant's culture—how they select people, how they structure and manage people's work, and how they use metrics and technology—amp up innovation and execution in ways that are hard for traditional companies to match.

I hear from many senior executives at traditional companies that are trying to reduce the number of organizational layers, which can be upward of seven or eight. I know of one hundred-billion-dollar company that had as many as fifteen layers. The CEO might direct the COO or CFO to take out one or two layers and increase the span of control of the remaining leaders. But cutting layers in itself does not fundamentally change how decisions are made.

Every company has cross-functional teams and other ways of coordinating what they do, but rarely are traditional companies organized to have teams that are on a single mission, accountable for the work from start to finish, including implementation and operation, and whose members work on nothing else. People do this teamwork while they are accountable for meeting the key performance indicators for their full-time job. In most cases, the cross-functional teams and standing committees are just layered over the existing organizational hierarchy. They don't replace it. The committees themselves can be very large (with as many as thirty to forty members) and cumbersome. They are slow in making necessary trade-offs.

Matrix reporting structures, in which people report to two different departments or functions, have been widely used to help align interests across functional silos. Some companies have a matrix within a matrix. But the complexity can create ambiguity and blur people's focus and accountability.

None of these approaches creates the speed and flexibility that a digital company can achieve. And none are specifically geared toward continuous innovation for the consumer. As a result, traditionally run businesses remain at a competitive disadvantage against a digital company in terms of keeping up with a fast-changing world.

They also fall short in attracting talent. Younger employees would rather be part of an autonomous team that is able to see an initiative or project through from start to finish. They want a sense of ownership of their work and are frustrated having to go through countless layers of approval and endless delays in order to do something. Those with technology skills that are in high demand ask about the work environment, as well as the company's stance on issues like sustainability and Me Too, and reject generous employment offers if they don't feel good about the workplace.

Of course, not every digital company is a model of organizational agility, and as Fidelity PI has shown, not every traditional company is doomed by the constructs that served it well in the past. What matters is embracing the factors that make a twenty-first-century social engine so hard to compete against: very few organizational layers, high-quality, high-velocity decision-making (in Jeff Bezos's vernacular), continuous innovation, superb execution, and a laser focus on aligning the company's efforts with serving the customer better.

Reinventing the Workplace at Fidelity Personal Investing

On a Sunday in the fall of 2014 I had a conversation with Kathy Murphy, president of Fidelity's Personal Investing unit, in the basement office of her home. When Murphy joined Fidelity PI in 2009, it was a leader in its businesses and had a rich heritage of providing excellent value to customers. PI continued to make strong progress to improve the customer experience by deepening relationships with clients and deploying technology. But she and I both remember that Sunday afternoon conversation well because it spurred in her a sense of urgency to make the kind of radical changes very few legacy companies attempt, let alone succeed at. She mustered the courage to transform the organizational structure and the culture, and today Fidelity PI runs as if it were a born-digital company.

"We were talking about the digital players around the world," Murphy recalls, "and a couple of things became very clear. First, they were moving very fast to appeal to customer segments in new ways, and second, the smaller digital companies were basically challenging the fundamental way the industry was approaching the market.

"We and most of our competitors were essentially product centric. While we had a strong client-service philosophy, the organization was structured around delivering products and services to those customers," she explained. "Growth was good versus traditional competitors, but it wasn't breakout growth. Meanwhile, disruptors were entering the space with a fresh perspective about what clients really value and how to simplify the overall customer experience using digital capabilities.

"So we had to challenge ourselves. We were a clear industry leader that had been very successful, but the world was changing. How could we add value to clients more quickly? How could we increase our speed? How could we reimagine the experience? And how could we expand the market itself?"

In many legacy companies, existing organizational hierarchy and culture get in the way of moving fast, and Fidelity PI was no exception. A time study provided insight into exactly why things bogged down. Murphy asked two of her direct reports to help analyze exactly how each person in one of PI's business units was actually spending their time. They found that on average each of the hundred people in that unit was working on ten different things at a given time. And those ten things were not the same across the entire group.

People worked in their various functional areas and passed things along when they had completed their part in a sequential stage-gate process. There were lots of large group meetings and PowerPoint decks to coordinate projects and stay aligned. "Business analysts" were deployed to coordinate between the business and technology functions. Some groups, like marketing, often were not involved until late in the development cycle. And if they had concerns at that stage—if they thought the idea wouldn't work—it meant the project would have to be reworked, creating significant slowdowns. Even simple things like scheduling meetings among a large group of very busy people could take weeks. Momentum and progress would get stalled.

Inspired by what digital companies were able to do, Murphy asked herself, "What if we organized ourselves more like the digital players do—using small, integrated teams aligned to achieve one customer objective at a time?"

That what-if led to a pilot project launched in the second half of 2016 in which the hundred people were broken into smaller teams of ten, each one charged with completing one objective at a time. The people on each team represented every type of expertise the project would require—technology, design, product development, regulatory compliance, marketing, and so forth. Together they would manage the project from start to finish. And each team member would work on nothing else.

The experimental integrated team achieved a 75 percent reduction in delivery time. That initial success kicked off the creation of more integrated teams. One was focused on digitizing customer service. The idea was to make it easy for clients to do on their own whatever they wanted to do on their own, such as check their account balance or adjust their portfolio, without having to call a service center. Like the initial pilot, this one also got the work accomplished much faster. Once team members were freed up from other work, they were able to make much more progress, faster, to simplify the customer experience.

Although the point was to create a better and more streamlined customer experience, the project generated two other benefits: It saved hundreds of millions of dollars for Fidelity and it allowed client-facing associates to work on activities that added more value in helping clients.

Clearly, Fidelity PI was onto something. Integrated teams were proving to be an effective way to accelerate innovation in the seventy-year-old company. And the people working on those agile-inspired teams found the new way of working liberating. They liked making many of their own decisions, without having to wade through layers of approvals, and eliminating the seemingly endless hours spent in meetings.

As people shared their excitement about the new way of

working, word spread through PI's informal company networks, and others who continued to do their jobs in the usual way started asking, "Why not us?" They, too, wanted to work in this exciting new way. "It got to where I was spending a lot of my time refereeing between those working in the new model and those outside it," Murphy says.

The feedback gave Murphy the impetus to transition the rest of the organization to the new way of working, quickly. She and her team came up with a new organizational design based on integrated teams wherever possible, and centered on something that is at the heart of every successful digital company: a deep knowledge of and unwavering focus on the end-to-end consumer experience.

From the Client Back to Organizational Structure

Murphy says she joined Fidelity in 2009 for three reasons: its values, including a customer-first mindset, the talented associate base, and Fidelity's forward-looking leadership. She knew Fidelity had a rich history of being a client-centric organization, and one that was comfortable challenging conventional wisdom. With support from the firm's senior management, she saw an opportunity to harness the culture in new ways to meet customers' changing needs and expectations after the 2007–09 recession.

To better understand customers' changing needs and expectations, Murphy and her leadership team tapped into the thousands of employees who had direct contact with customers and took great pride in serving them well. She brought groups of them to the home office, where a series of "summits" gave the senior team a chance to hear first-hand what those associates had been observing about customers in their everyday interactions. She made many visits to field sites, where she encouraged people to be candid about customer feedback, and listened to hours of recorded customer calls (and still does—twenty hours per month).

Meanwhile, digital companies like Amazon, Netflix, and Google were interacting with customers in entirely new ways and raising customer expectations. Against that backdrop, Fidelity PI's efforts to fix the problems it had surfaced didn't seem good enough. They had to understand their clients in greater granularity and depth and use that deep understanding to drive all their decisions. In 2014, a team began the arduous process of describing in great detail the first of several customer design personas that represented the key client segments PI served. "Susie," for example, was thirty-seven and a half years old, digitally savvy, with a little bit of investing experience. She was married with two kids, lived outside Philadelphia, and took the train to work. She used her mobile device often. It was quite intentional that Susie was female, as women have been largely underserved by the financial services industry. She represented a tremendous opportunity to challenge current industry practices.

The team researched every aspect of Susie's life and every step of her day. Her life was mapped out on a twenty-foot stretch of wall covered with charts and dozens of Post-its. The pain points in her customer journey were identified, as were the metrics associated with them. One set of bullet points captured the priorities in Susie's financial life. Another charted the chronology of her interactions with Fidelity as she accessed her account. One section of wall assessed the business impact of various changes in the customer experience and over time. Another section tracked all of the tasks team members were trying to complete and how their timing would affect—and be affected by—other projects. The bits of handwritten notes could easily be moved or modified as things progressed or ran into problems. It is someone's full-time job to curate the wall and keep it up-to-date.

Everyone in the PI business was expected to know Susie's persona, to effectively "walk in her high heels," as Murphy put it. The wall made all of the details about Susie and the projects that were geared toward her visible for all to see.

I have seen other companies undertake this kind of exercise, but rarely with the energy and attention to detail of the Fidelity PI team. It is common to delegate the task to consulting firms. When internal people do the digging, however, the learning tends to be deeper and people are more attuned to the fine points that can be differentiators. It is more than conducting focus groups; it is keenly observing to note the specifics of consumer behavior.

Once Susie's journey was completed, the team did the same exercise for "Sally," a widow who lived in Scottsdale, Arizona. Sally is older, closer to retirement, and has more complex financial needs than Susie.

That left a third broad category of customer: Harry, an active trader.

Those three personas, Susie, Sally, and Harry, became the reference points for mapping the end-to-end customer experiences of three major segments of customers. It was expected that these client archetypes would be at the forefront in every discussion of a new initiative and every business decision.

They also became the basis for restructuring the organization into some 180 integrated teams and collapsing an organization of up to eight layers between the front line and the Fidelity PI president into just three.

Fidelity's organization structure now looks remarkably like that of a digital company. Having observed the company for six years, I can say that it has gained the same competitive advantage as a result. After working that way for one full year, releases of new products, features, and services increased by 50 percent year over year. In addition, PI achieved record revenues and profits, increased its market share, and widened the distance between itself and other competitors in their space. In year two there was an additional 130 percent improvement in the number of new releases, further accelerating progress.

"Working from the customer back, we reimagined what the client experience should be and how it could be individualized in ways that are impossible to deliver if you're not digital," Murphy says. "We have been able to add a lot more value to clients."

One example is Fidelity ZERO. "Our CEO wanted us to accelerate innovation, and we had the idea to offer index funds with zero fees," Murphy told me. "We looked at our financials and thought we could do it. The CEO gave us the go-ahead in mid-May of 2018 and we were ready to launch it in six weeks. The only delay was waiting for regulatory approval. The day we launched, it caused a 5 percent decline in the stock price of our competitors."

That initiative was part of a steady stream of new features, new experiences, and new products introduced at a much faster pace. They are helping to democratize investing, which is bringing services to a broader audience and effectively expanding the market space along the lines of '10x, meaning that the total potential market could be many times larger than it is now.

Agile and Just Three Layers

Even a quintessential digital company like Amazon has a multilayer reporting structure in some parts of its business, such as its warehouse operations and Marketplace for third-party vendors. But in areas where innovation for customers is most crucial, *teams* rule the day, and the number of layers from CEO Jeff Bezos to the team is fewer than four.

As Fidelity PI experimented with, then expanded, its integrated team-based structure, they used the principles and language of agile development (my view is that the principles are more important than specific terminology). Work is organized into domains, which is agile-speak for areas focused on a particular strategic objective. Wealth Management is one (this is the realm of "Sally's" end-to-end journey); Digital Planning ("Susie's" realm) is another. One domain is focused on getting the business off a mainframe and onto the cloud, and another comprises parts of the business that are better run in a traditional way, such as the sales force and back office.

The work of the domain is divided into tribes, each of which focuses on an objective that its domain is trying to fulfill. "Wealth Management," for example, has nine tribes for focus areas such as "Wealth Planning" and "Retirement and Income Solutions." The work of a tribe is further separated into specific issues or problems that need to be solved. This is where the integrated teams of ten to fifteen people, also known as squads, come in. Wealth Management has about sixty of them.

The organizational layers below Murphy, then, are few in number: domains, tribes, and squads.

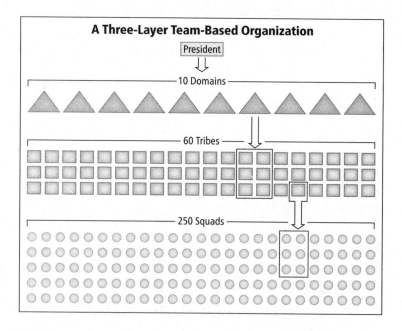

A Three-Layer Team-Based Organization

President

10 Domains

60 Tribes

250 Squads

The increased speed is the result of having people in the squads completely dedicated, integrated, and co-located where possible, giving them a sharply defined mission and allowing them the autonomy to find their own solutions to the problem or task assigned to them. At Fidelity, floors once lined with cubicles are now open spaces with high and low tables for people to prop their laptops on or gather around for a conversation. Murphy no longer has an office but rather a standing desk in a corner of the floor.

The environment is appealing not only to millennials and to technologists, whom Fidelity has to compete for against the likes of Google and Facebook, but also to most frontline associates, who say they appreciate the greater empowerment, collaboration, and speed. "When the person is sitting right next to you, you get the feedback right away," explains Ram Subramanian, who leads PI's Wealth Management domain. With over $1 trillion in assets, Wealth Management is Fidelity's largest domain. Subramanian continues, "You don't have to wait eight weeks to hear that something won't work."

Coordination and control are age-old problems at big companies. But the digital start-ups and giants have proven that technology goes a long way in solving them. You could say there are *zero* organizational layers when technology makes information transparent to everyone who is authorized to see it.

Following a push to recruit one hundred highly skilled data scientists and technologists from companies like Microsoft and Amazon, Fidelity gave fifteen of them the task of building a platform that would allow information to flow up, down, and across the organization. It took just three months to create the Sensors Dashboard, which measures activities in all parts of PI on a real-time basis and can be accessed by all the squads.

For managing projects and agile teams, Fidelity PI uses the popular third-party software application Jira. It tracks information from the bottom up, flagging anything that is falling behind so the team can take the initiative to address it.

Another third-party software product called Jira Align (formerly AgileCraft) helps top-level leaders centralize the plan and link it to execution throughout the organization. It keeps the big picture front and center, even as it is broken into discrete tasks and missions that are assigned to teams, and it predicts a team's progress on its task. Anyone in the system can go in and check on things—to see, for example, how a particular squad is performing, their backlog, their degree of satisfaction, and their speed. It makes it easy to find the dependencies, where the work of one squad is dependent on the work of someone else's, so people can adjust their priorities and do their own self-policing.

Technology makes real-time data transparent, but still, the organization depends on people to knit the pieces together on a daily basis. How? Through good old-fashioned human interaction.

Scrum masters—people who are expert in the methodologies and rituals of agile—facilitate daily stand-ups, fifteen-minute meetings so brief that no chairs are necessary. They are not project leaders. Instead, they help the squad align on the objective and timing, help identify dependencies and remove obstacles to the squad's progress, and help the team stay on track.

A cadre of agile coaches works with tribe leaders to help ensure that the work of the tribes comes together to support the higher-level objectives. They are expert in implementing agile projects and provide ongoing coaching to the tribes. In the early days of implementing agile, they play an important role in educating leaders. As these agile skills mature, these coaches help leaders and teams leverage the benefits of agile in more sophisticated ways.

Coordination is also facilitated through "big room planning." Once a quarter, the top hundred leaders gather in a room to review all of their interdependencies. Those sessions were a bit cumbersome at the start, consuming two full days. Now that people are accustomed to zeroing in on the potential conflicts, the sessions are typically several hours long. People are energized by the decisiveness of resolving conflicts on the spot.

The Soft Side of Digital Competitors

Metrics and digital dashboards can help keep people's efforts aligned, but people's greatest potential is released when they see how their work impacts some bigger purpose. Having a sense of ownership of one's work is a huge source of satisfaction in a person's life. Working with leaders who remove the obstacles and resolve the conflicts takes that satisfaction to a higher level.

When Fidelity PI began piloting its cross-functional

teams, the participants adapted to it quickly. Unlike the usual stories about employees resisting change, at Fidelity most people welcomed it. And that social acceptance preceded any edict from the top.

By mid-2017 it was clear that PI needed to accelerate the time frame for getting others in the organization working in the new team-based organization structure. Murphy called on Monish Kumar, managing director and senior partner at Boston Consulting Group, and his team to help get it done by the end of the year. Murphy knew that her organization was ready for the change, and she was totally committed to it. Kumar recalls getting a phone call from her on the Fourth of July and thinking, "She clearly has things besides a summer barbecue on her mind!"

Murphy set January 2018 as the target date for Project Snap the Line. "We wanted to start 2018 with a fresh start, no looking back," Murphy said. Kumar embraced the power of Murphy's transformative vision and drew up plans to deliver the change that was needed in a very aggressive time frame.

They took a customer-centric approach to designing the organization structure, diagrammed the domains, tribes, and squads, and educated people about how it would work. "We moved beyond the traditional product and functional organizational structure to one defined largely by the needs of customers, intentionally reinforcing a customer-obsessed mindset," Murphy explained.

But success ultimately hinged on the human interactions within the teams, and that depended critically on the team leaders.

Most of today's digital giants started with a small team of highly skilled individuals whose talents were in high demand. Companies competed for those people (and still do) in part by offering stock options and in part by creating a great work environment. The perks and freedoms of Silicon Valley may grab attention, but they reflect fundamentally different assumptions that digital companies make about people and how best to lead them.

The prevailing assumption is that most people are inherently self-motivated, want to contribute, can solve problems, and have the desire to learn new things. They want to be heard, respected, and treated fairly and know that their inputs matter. A boss with a command-and-control leadership style is likely to drive them right into the arms of a recruiter.

It was critically important that PI's leaders were chosen in large part based on their ability to foster collaboration among knowledge workers, empower their teams, and be supportive of their squads and chapters. PI had already embraced the concept of leadership based on "multiplying" behaviors, as described in *Multipliers* by Liz Wiseman. The PI senior team now used these concepts to create a guide for choosing the leaders of the tribes, chapter areas, squads, and teams.

None of the existing leaders were guaranteed a job of leading a tribe or squad. Instead, they, along with everyone else, were invited to apply.

Then Murphy and her senior team put a tremendous amount of time and effort into ensuring that they chose the right people for every one of the new team leader positions.

Every leader went through a 360-degree review, and two se-nior leaders interviewed every candidate, an extensive pro-cess that took about a month of very focused effort by the whole PI senior team.

Then it was time to choose. The PI senior team locked themselves in a room for two full days and evenings to pore over all of the information they had gathered. They had the results of the 360-degree reviews, performance histories, and meticulous notes from interviews for fifteen hundred people who had shown interest in becoming a leader. "We had everything up on the wall and talked about every single person in depth," Murphy says.

"We knew that who we picked as team leaders was a test of whether we were serious about changing the way we work," she continued. "And that forced us to make some really tough choices.

"The process was heavily weighted toward whether they could lead in the new way, not what they knew. So we held up each person against the multiplying leadership traits we had defined. It became clear that some of the people who had been considered heroes and didn't do anything wrong wouldn't be able to make it in the new model. Some could, but others just weren't suited to it."

"On the other hand," says Subramanian, "we found some gems. Some people didn't know much about the ac-tual product but were very good about helping people col-laborate and building an output that was customer focused. About a third of the squad leaders would never have been chosen in the old system."

The senior leaders chose the tribe leaders first, and then

the squad leaders, and got some early reassurance from the ranks. "I knew we were on the right track when someone on a squad approached me shortly after we announced our selections and made a telling comment," Murphy recalls. "This person said, 'I wasn't sure you were serious, but then when I saw you pick Kate, I knew it was for real.'" Kate, Murphy explained, was soft-spoken and not your typical alpha personality. She ended up getting one of the most desirable positions and doing a great job.

All of Fidelity Personal Investing converted to the new way of working by January 3, 2018. Murphy is quick to say it is still a work in process. In the early months, they had to clarify that empowerment doesn't mean that teams are completely autonomous. They have to ensure that their work is aligned with others' and that it is time-bound. Very few people left the organization, voluntarily or otherwise, and by the end of that year, the vast majority of employees said they would never want to go back to the old way of working.

Soon after PI fully implemented agile, other Fidelity business units, and even some staff departments such as Internal Audit, began their own transition to this integrated team-based structure. Now many parts of Fidelity operate that way.

The "Who" and "How" of a Social Engine: Leadership and Culture

It makes sense that integrated teams are able to complete projects faster, but today's digital giants gain more potent benefits from their social engines. Consider Amazon's ability to branch out into new areas and scale up fast. Sure, we know that Jeff Bezos has a fertile imagination and immense talent, but the company's success cannot be attributed to one individual.

Amazon has an army of people searching for new things, striving to improve on what already exists, and continually raising the bar on their own performance. Every job candidate is expected to have the highest standards, and a desire to learn and think big. Amazon's hiring process routinely includes certified "bar raisers," people who have demonstrated their ability to assess whether the applicant's talent is above Amazon's current average. Employees are also expected to be "builders" and idea generators, committed to creating something of intrinsic value.

A critical mass of such people organized and managed in a way that releases their energy and talent is an awesome force of nature. In describing the origins of AWS, Amazon's fast-growing Web services business, Andy Jassy paints a picture of smart people pooling their ideas in an environment conducive to developing them into something new. Jassy, who has led AWS from its start, says the germ of the idea came at a retreat at Jeff Bezos's house in 2003, three years before AWS was launched with intentionally little fanfare.

As Ron Miller reported in *TechCrunch* in July 2016, Amazon's executive team was conducting an exercise to identify the company's core competencies when the discussion expanded:

"As the team worked, Jassy recalled, they realized they had also become quite good at running infrastructure services like compute, storage and database. . . . What's more, they had become highly skilled at running reliable, scalable, cost-effective data centers out of need. . . . It was at that point, without even fully articulating it, that they started to formulate the idea of what AWS could be, and they began to wonder if they had an additional business providing infrastructure services to developers.

" 'In retrospect it seems fairly obvious, but at the time I don't think we had ever really internalized that,' Jassy explained."

The power of any company's social engine lies in both the *who* and the *how*. Who do you hire? Or in Fidelity's case, who do you select to be the team leaders? And how do you enhance their natural instincts to do meaningful work?

The founders of today's fast-growing technology companies, even going back to Bill Gates and Steve Jobs in the early days of their companies, put tremendous effort into recruiting people. They considered people not just for how well they fit into an immediate job slot but for their ability to strive, to learn, to grow, and to get things done.

Google cofounders Sergey Brin and Eric Schmidt established standards every new candidate had to meet and a process for upholding that standard, including the need for final approval from a central reviewer. Over time, cofounder Larry Page assumed that role of giving final approval to every new hire.

Google executives also took an active role in amassing

top talent, as Laszlo Bock, former head of Google's "people operations," explained to me in 2016: "We all spent one and a half to two days a week recruiting. And not just interviewing but selling candidates, cultivating people, getting to know them, building relationships over time, and sometimes over years until somebody was ready to move.

"The goal was to hire people who were overqualified for every job, in terms of experience or attributes and to disqualify anyone who gave even a small signal that they might not be collaborative or intellectually humble," Bock continued. "Whatever the job, we looked for what we called *emergent leadership*. When an issue came up, would the person step in to fill that void, and perhaps more importantly, relinquish power to somebody else in a different phase of the problem?"

When Jeff Bezos lured Jeff Wilke to Amazon from AlliedSignal (now Honeywell) in 1999, Wilke was metrics-driven, customer-oriented, and a doer—the kind of person who would carry cardboard boxes full of books despite having had fast-track growth potential at his former employer. He thrived on the expectations for high standards, a sense of ownership, and thinking big that had already taken root as key elements of Amazon's culture. He brought with him knowledge of the operating tools that Larry Bossidy had used to drive superb execution at AlliedSignal (the subject of *Execution,* which Bossidy and I co-authored). Wilke helped drive the company's growth, as he grew, too, in his career. He is now CEO of Worldwide Consumer at the $232 billion company.

Digital giants expect people to be idea generators, problem solvers, team players, and learners. At Netflix, for example, the stated expectations for salaried employees are not what you would see among most Fortune 500 companies. They explicitly include things like "You create new ideas that prove useful," "You inspire others with your thirst for excellence," "You are ego-less when searching for the best ideas," and "You learn rapidly and eagerly." These traits are recurring themes in the digital world. They guide hiring decisions, and their frequent repetition helps shape the culture.

A simple way to define that amorphous term *culture* is the expression of shared values through common behaviors. A critical mass of people behaving in a certain way shapes the behavior of others, so the behavior of those who get hired and assigned to positions of influence is immensely important. That's why Murphy and her team put so much time and effort into choosing the tribe and chapter leaders.

Once established, the culture becomes a magnet for others who share those values and behave that way—for example, for those who care more about learning and contributing than accumulating power by whatever means. It becomes self-perpetuating.

For traditional companies, the expectation for continuous learning and curiosity (another of Netflix's stated expectations) is a paradigm shift in thinking about an individual's career path. In most companies, people wait to take the next step up in their vertical silo—marketing, finance, sales, IT. In an organization with just three layers, however, a relatively small number of people will make a leap to a higher organizational level. For most, progress is marked in other ways, such as building deeper expertise, broader perspective, or greater ability to deal with complexity.

When Fidelity PI moved more than five thousand of its people out of functional silos and onto integrated teams, it needed to address the approaches to career progression associated with the traditional corporate hierarchy. The new model with many fewer layers focuses on how associates can contribute to adding value and having a positive impact on the client and the business on a continuous basis. People are rewarded for how much they contribute and how much their skills and expertise can grow. Associates liked the new way of working but worried about how they would advance in their career and what "promotions" or pay increases would be based on. The organization addressed this by focusing on skills, expertise, and personal development as ways to mark meaningful career growth and advancement.

Fidelity PI's new organizational structure includes "chapters" (borrowed from agile methodology), which are basically areas of expertise. The people on a squad are drawn from various chapters.

Chapter leaders have the responsibility to help set the strategy for the tribes, develop the skills and expertise of their people, and coach their performance on an ongoing basis.

"We now have a detailed skills matrix for all the disci-

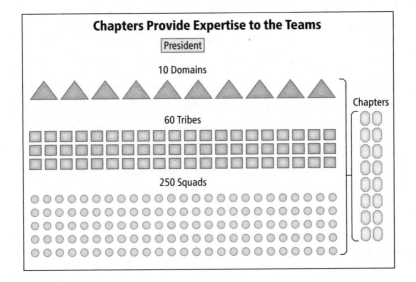

plines in our organization (different aspects of technology, digital, user design, marketing, and so on) that gives people a path forward for broadening their skill sets and advancing," Murphy explains. "It also provides context by showing what other squads you could work on to deploy and broaden your skills in different squads or even different chapters by acquiring new skills."

The skills assessment and matrix give people a framework for progressing. "It is sort of the new currency in terms of how we pay people and how you progress in your career," Murphy adds. "Some people want to develop in their career by leading and coaching people, while others would much rather be rewarded for the hands-on value they provide to customers and the business and for deepening their expertise."

Fidelity PI has made a major commitment to the development of its people and their skills by having a "learning day" every week. Every Tuesday people are free to work on developing new or existing skills, taking classes, or doing whatever else they want to do to learn and grow. That accounts for 20 percent of their time. And Fidelity PI's people do take advantage of it, to the tune of a million hours of learning in total the first year the practice was established.

Leaders are expected to keep learning, too. The top two hundred people at Fidelity PI took classes at MIT to learn about basic algorithms. Subramanian is learning from scratch how to code in Python. And some of the experts in mainframe technology got certified in cloud computing.

Murphy says, "The emphasis on learning absolutely has accelerated our innovation and digital journey."

Turbocharging Creativity

If there is a secret sauce that makes the various components of a company's social engine—things like minimal organizational layers, integrated autonomous teams, transparency, and individual growth—even more powerful, it is this: the power of *simultaneous dialogue*.

Imagine an integrated team of experts whose natural inclination is to learn, grow, and strive. They are focused on a crystal-clear mission they believe in and for which there are specific performance metrics. Their work is unimpeded by politicking or bureaucracy and helped by a leader who clears the path.

When these people are discussing something as a group,

every member hears every comment simultaneously and therefore without distortion. As information is shared, unconscious biases get checked, and a *single source of truth,* or shared reality, emerges.

With that single source of truth as a foundation, the continued back-and-forth is a kind of triangulation process for ascertaining the best idea, solution, or option. I refer to the output of this kind of *simultaneous dialogue* as the bull's-eye, because it is the group's central focus and purpose.

Insights develop as people share observations and information, building on each other's comments. New information and insights stimulate other new ideas, create new energy, and expand people's mental capacity. This is where new ideas are hatched and, with real-time data and feedback, can be quickly iterated and refined.

The dialogue can generate successful innovations and breakthroughs in solving problems very fast. Especially in large organizations, the output of one team is the input to another's, so the effect can be cumulative. This is the social engine that powers a start-up and creates value for the customer, the business, and employees all at once.

With vigilance to keep it working well, this kind of social engine can accelerate a digital company's growth and extend its lead. Traditional or legacy companies should not underestimate its power or importance.

Fidelity PI's transition to be a digital innovator should encourage every aspiring leader. You, too, can do it! Whether you are creating a digital company, transforming to become one, or are already in one, your leadership will shape the company's competitive advantage—or put the business at a competitive disadvantage. The next chapter crystallizes the key characteristics any leader needs to take their company into the future.

CHAPTER 8

LEADERS WHO CREATE WHAT'S NEXT

Rule #6: Leaders continuously learn, imagine, and break through obstacles to create the change that other companies must contend with.

Following the new rules without paying attention to your own leadership is dangerous. Companies are created, expanded, allowed to wither and die, or get revived by their leaders. Walmart started to digitize in 2001 but those efforts didn't go anywhere until Doug McMillon became CEO in 2014. Microsoft was treading water until Satya Nadella took over. Larry Page and Sergey Brin created a new competitive field. So did Mark Zuckerberg. These are reminders of what should be obvious: that leadership matters to the success of a business.

We are now in a period when leaders are tested continuously against changing conditions and against each other. Digital leaders so far have an edge, not because they are younger and tech savvy but because they lead in ways that are inherently better suited to a digital company in the digital age.

Understanding what is different about digital leaders will help everyone who has been successful in a traditional setting and must now change their habits and mental gears. It might sound harsh, but those who find they do not match up against what leadership demands in the digital age should consider taking a different role and clearing the path for someone else. Rupert Murdoch of Twenty-First Century Fox and Frank Lowy of Westfield Corp. conceded all or part of their businesses to others who were presumably better suited to run them. More of these leadership changes will come.

But no one is predestined for success or failure. It is an open game, and we are seeing the challenge to current leaders playing out in real time.

Take the Walt Disney Company, an American icon. Bob Iger became its CEO in 2005 following a decades-long career in broadcast television. The company pumped out a more than respectable EPS and dividend for many years under his leadership. But as media watchers saw Netflix taking off, they saw no discernible match from Disney. Some began to question how and when Disney would respond to the steepening decline of broadcast and rise of video streaming.

For much of Iger's tenure, he had sought to reinvigorate the company's content production, especially animation, which had lost its mojo. The most direct path to refreshing Disney's creativity, he believed, was to acquire Pixar, which had been wielding its creative and technology skill to produce everyone's new animation favorites, including *Toy Story* and *Finding Nemo*. Iger made the persuasive case to Steve Jobs that a deal would be good for Pixar and Disney, Jobs agreed, and the deal was finalized in 2006.

The pursuit of quality content led to two other major acquisitions that soon followed: Marvel Entertainment in 2009, with its library of comic book characters, and Lucasfilm in 2012, with its Star Wars franchise.

The acquisitions lit Disney's box-office success on fire. In 2016 (also the year Shanghai Disneyland opened), four new releases generated more than $1 billion each in worldwide box-office receipts.

Still, while digital technology had been on Iger's watch list for many years, there was no indication that the media giant was taking video streaming seriously. Until 2017. Suddenly Iger's references to disruption and digital technology led to action. Disney jumped into video streaming in a big way.

BAMTech, a Manhattan-based start-up created to stream live baseball games, would be key. It had built Hulu's streaming service, as well as HBO Now's and others'. Disney had earlier made a small investment in the company; then, in 2017, it negotiated to expand its stake to 75 percent. BAMTech built a streaming service for Disney-owned ESPN that launched in 2018, and another, which we now know as Disney+, that launched in late 2019. Having BAMTech build the digital platform was faster than building it in-house but required a commitment of $1.5 billion.

That dollar amount was small in comparison to what

became another piece in the Disney digital puzzle. In mid-2017, shortly after Disney expanded its BAMTech investment, Rupert Murdoch opened a conversation with Iger about Twenty-First Century Fox assets. That got Iger and his strategy chief, Kevin Mayer, thinking about which parts of Fox could enhance Disney's offerings and increase its scale. Fox's movie studios and presence in India's growing market would be major boosts to Disney's global expansion. Fox also had a sizable stake in Hulu, which would add to Disney's shares and give it majority control of a third streaming service that could distribute content not suited to the Disney+ family-friendly brand.

Negotiations followed, and the Fox deal closed in 2019 with Disney taking on yet another big acquisition and financial commitment—to the tune of $71 billion—in the midst of the transition to streaming that was already under way. By the end of 2019, Iger had placed his bets and committed tens of billions of dollars to connect directly with consumers and ensure an ample supply of quality content. Disney had begun to reclaim the content it had licensed to other companies, eliminating a reliable source of revenues. And it established a price of $6.99 a month for Disney+, low enough to appeal to average families.

All of those decisions meant that earnings and cash would take a hit in the short term and the moneymaking model would change. Instead of earnings per share, Iger focused on the number of subscribers as the more important measure of performance.

Iger made his case convincingly to investors and had

to do the same for those inside the company. The old moneymaking model was being disrupted and so was the organization. A new group was formed to create content specifically for the direct-to-consumer market. New business segments, with labels such as "Direct-to-consumer and international" and "Parks, experiences, and consumer products," reflected the new orientation and separated the creators from the data crunchers. To bring Disney employees, investors, and consumers along, Iger traveled the globe to explain Disney's plans and to listen. And he got the board to support a new incentive structure.

So, is Iger a digital leader? It was not a given that Iger would adapt to the tenets of competitive advantage in the digital age, given his experience and background. Any leader coming of age in a stable business environment and especially those in a company that has been dominant, if not monopolistic, can struggle to adjust to the dynamics that exist today. But he seems to have followed the new rules:

- Seeing what consumers value most: great content, lovable characters, and new ways to consume entertainment
- Using a digital platform to connect with and learn about individual consumers with the potential to personalize their connection with Disney characters and stories
- Creating a moneymaking model that focuses on building scale

- Engaging eco-partners—such as Verizon, offering Disney+ to its customers—to scale up the number of subscribers
- Changing the social engine to support the company's new positioning and moneymaking model

As CEO, Iger seemed to think and act like many of the digital leaders I have observed. He had an open mind; kept learning and discerning new patterns; and was imagining something new, thinking big, and steering the organization to boldly pursue it despite the risks. In short, he had the mindset, skills, and courage to lead in the digital era.

Any company that is or wants to be digital must have leaders who match up against the criteria a digital company requires. Iger was not expected to be a digital leader when Disney's board of directors gave him the CEO job in 2005, but by the time he announced his retirement on February 25, 2020, he had become one. The same can be said of B2W's Anna Saicali and Fidelity's Kathy Murphy, both of whom developed their careers in traditional companies and became digital leaders.

What Is a Digital Leader?

The most significant differences I see in the leaders of digital companies versus the leaders of traditional or legacy companies have to do with their cognition, skills, and psychological orientation. What is particularly relevant is how these things blend together to link big-picture thinking with pragmatic matters of moneymaking, execution, and speed. Each of the descriptions below captures an aspect of how digital leaders succeed.

- They have the mental capacity to think in terms of 10x or 100x, to imagine a future space that doesn't exist, and the confidence that they will overcome whatever obstacles they might encounter. They are knowledgeable about and supremely focused on the customer and have the imagination and vision to conceive of an end-to-end customer experience and a large-scale future space. They can see how the moneymaking and the company's ecosystem will work together in new and sustainable ways. They are willing to make big bets and to withstand initial losses of profits and cash amid doubts and skepticism from Wall Street, because they have a clear picture in their mind of how things will work. They are able to build ecosystems on an enormous scale and believe every market they enter is expandable.
- They have a facility for and are comfortable with data-based analysis. Facts and knowledge—not predictable outcomes—give them the courage to act. They blend data with intuition, examine future trends, and adjust their actions and offerings as new data and facts emerge.
- There is a fluidity to their thinking. They welcome change and even seek it. They are in fact the source of what others perceive as relentless change. People talk about how digital companies are disrupting indus-

tries, but most of their leaders don't start with that intention. They are motivated to create something new. Their fluid, iterative thought process makes the once-a-year strategy review obsolete. Instead, it is ongoing.

- They are hungry for what's next and are willing to create and destroy. Their psychology is geared toward high speed, urgency, and continuous experimentation. They constantly search for what can be improved and what can be created that could be important to consumers and provide a new source of revenue. They are not afraid to cannibalize what they have or abandon what isn't working. While legacy company leaders expect a formal presentation with every "i" dotted and every "t" crossed before they approve an initiative, digital leaders are willing to make big bets without the formal apparatus. They focus on the customer benefits and allow for uncertainty. Their psychology, habits, and DNA are predisposed to explore, experiment, learn, and adjust, and to quickly cut losses when necessary.

- They have the observational acumen to absorb hard data and piece together what does not yet exist.

- AI and algorithms can help digitally adept companies sort out operational complexity, but the leaders of these companies must be able to juggle many variables as they change the basic components of their business. They are not overwhelmed by the speed of change and are comfortable with the concept of creating MVPs, or minimal viable products—a goodenough version of an offering that can be tested and iterated quickly based on customer feedback. Their ability to handle the constant flood of new information allows them to react quickly to the speed of social media and word of mouth, and to continually look to shift resources and rebalance short-term and long-term goals.

- This kind of fluid thinking and ease in taking in new and complex information goes hand in hand with continuous learning. Such leaders stay abreast of what is new and challenge themselves to learn about things they know nothing about.

- They are literate in the application of algorithmic science and value fact-based reasoning. But they know that data is not always sufficient.

- They rely on metrics and transparent data to drive execution. They are highly disciplined in ensuring that their people deliver results on time.

- They are skilled in selecting the right people for the right jobs and are quick to move people to other positions who are not suited to the job as it changes.

- They are willing to reconceptualize the organizational structure so that decision-making takes place closer to the customer to improve the speed and quality of decisions. They are comfortable giving those under them the freedom to act, while using data and incentives to increase accountability and execution.

- The word *courage* has been associated with strong leadership throughout history in every walk of life, from war to sports to politics. For digital leaders or traditional leaders becoming digital, courage has a specific granularity. They have the courage to act decisively, often making bold moves despite the fact that the emerging landscape is often based on incomplete information and unknowns. Their courage and boldness come from their ability to take in and sort through a flood of new data and information, combined with the raw nerve to take risks.

This final bullet is certainly true of Bob Iger, who entered the streaming race later than many expected. He took on a lot of debt to buy Fox and Hulu, knowing full well that pricing could be a race to the bottom, while incurring heavy cash expenditures that will reduce earnings and could invite attacks from the media, investors, and activists. If the repositioning of Disney proves to be untenable, it could damage the Disney brand as well as Iger's reputation. But Iger had the cognitive ability to figure out a path for Disney and the sheer nerve to place a big bet on it.

Tests of Leadership

Today's fast-paced digital economy is not an era for the timid. But leaders who take bold action without having the requisite skills are merely reckless.

When leaders fail it is usually because their business skills do not fit the challenges of the job. Poor judgment in allocating cash and the failure to hire and train the necessary talent are common shortcomings. For example, we know that autonomous (or self-driving) vehicles (AVs) are coming in the near future, but no one knows when, where, how quickly they will be adopted, and who will dominate. Companies in that space will rise or fall based on how well their leaders can navigate the fog of uncertainty in that emerging market space.

AVs depend on huge amounts of data, and their development entails a great deal of risk. As we've already seen, accidents in the testing and development phase can have an outsize impact on consumer acceptance. Some leaders are pursuing AVs aggressively despite the risk, while others are moving more cautiously.

Ecosystems will inevitably compete against each other, and mistakes here, including moving too slowly, may be an existential threat. Leaders have to imagine how the moving parts will fit together, build the relationships, and be comfortable sharing information with eco-partners, versus going it alone, as they are accustomed.

The total revenue of the global mobility market is unknown, but total car ownership is in decline worldwide. Leaders vying to compete in that space will have to find a moneymaking model that works. That is an especially big challenge for leaders of traditional automakers. Ford, for one, has a cash problem. Will its CEO partner with other carmakers and get the Ford board comfortable with that arrangement? Will cash constraints make it hard to create a broad enough ecosystem to stay competitive? Ford is testing AVs in three cities, while most other automakers are testing in just one. Ford stands to benefit by getting data from varied settings, but can it afford to do so for an extended period of time? The CEO has to be willing to shift resources as necessary, withstand a barrage of criticism over suppressed earnings, and have the skills to deftly explain the narrative to investors and employees.

These are business issues leaders in the auto industry have to reckon with. And their decisions have serious consequences. Note the turnover in the CEO positions at BMW, Ford, and Daimler.

Bob Chapek, who succeeded Iger as Disney CEO in February 2020, will have to weather whatever impact the new moneymaking model has on the cost of capital. Disney's stock price was holding up well at the end of 2019 in light of high initial subscription numbers for Disney+, but it was unclear if those subscription numbers were sustainable and if investors would accept lower earnings per share. In 2018, Disney earnings estimates for 2020 were $8.20. By late 2019, estimates for 2020 had fallen below $6.

Will CEO Reed Hastings be able to continue to attract funding for Netflix as the competitive landscape shifts? Netflix's continued success depends on Hastings's ability to keep the moneymaking model working, even as other companies attempt to lure consumers away with new entertainment options. Netflix has been able to raise prices in recent years without significant blowback. Would the company become unattractive to funders if Hastings lowered prices at some point to attract new subscribers? In April 2020, on the heels of adding 15.8 million new subscriptions in the first quarter and having positive cash flow for the first time in six years largely because of a slowdown in production,

Netflix announced that it was raising $1 billion in low-cost debt split between euros and dollars.

Cultivating Digital Leaders

Leadership obsolescence is a reality. Many leaders in traditional companies developed their cognitive skills around incrementalism versus rapid and exponential growth. Many used price increases or acquisitions to boost revenues rather than to create new market spaces (note Procter & Gamble's pattern of premium pricing and Disney's price increases at its theme parks). Many lack technology skills and knowledge to survive in today's landscape or may have a weaker appetite for risk.

Understandably, it is hard for them to imagine what technology makes possible and to enthusiastically drive exponential growth. They may have no experience in building relationships with eco-partners and no exposure to the power of a digital platform. Most leaders in positions of power in legacy companies have come up through functional or vertical silos—from marketing, finance, or operations. If they started at the bottom, they had to rise up six layers or more. That kind of career progression gives them little if any consumer experience or few opportunities to build their business savvy. Even leaders who have run a profit and loss unit probably did so without balance sheet responsibility and may be handicapped in trying to conceive moneymaking models that are suited to the digital age.

Up-and-coming leaders had to fight for resources, play politics, and be evaluated based on how well they met the numbers. Reviews in legacy companies are largely focused on the rearview mirror. Some had performance metrics around customer satisfaction or a Net Promoter Score index, which are not forward-looking metrics and do not reflect imagination or vision.

Leaders who came up through consulting firms had their DNA shaped by analyzing multiple industries and massaging facts to get meaningful insights. They tend to be very good in cutting through internal and external data and can often see the big picture. But a large percentage ultimately fail because they lack experience managing a large organization or building top teams, or because of their personality. Their expertise and intelligence allow them to think they are the smartest person in the room. But as a result, they stop listening and are unable to develop and steer the company's social engine.

Turnover among CEO leaders at traditional companies will likely increase. A good percentage will find it near impossible to convert their mindset and skills or will be unable to do so fast enough. Traditional companies intent on transforming into digital ones should consider whether their leaders can make the shift. If not, they may need leaders from the outside. Amazon has become a talent factory and a popular source for recruiting.

At the same time, companies that do a deeper search might unearth potential digital leaders in their midst. I have observed a number of situations, beyond those at Fidelity,

B2W, and Disney, where a leader from a traditional company put the organization on a digital trajectory.

Leadership "potential" should be based on the qualities that digital leaders share: a basic knowledge of algorithms, a customer orientation, and business savvy, as well as personal leadership traits such as imagination and a drive to execute. In particular, the blend of skills and personal traits must result in good judgment.

People can learn and change. I have seen experienced executives at the highest levels of traditional organizations eagerly learning what platforms, algorithms, and data can do for their company, and the scope of their thinking and imagination has been enlarged. Some of these leaders now believe that achieving 10x growth is possible, whereas they did not before. They are able to imagine satisfying a customer need that stretches out further in time, seven years or more, and have begun to experiment and test what that market space could be. They know that competition is inevitable and are learning to experiment faster and accept some failures.

Millennials represent a richer vein of leadership hope for the future, but they may need to develop their social skills. Those with a background in computer science can nail coding and platform and app development. But their thinking has a downside. It is binary. Such experience can condition people to see things in black and white. They may lack empathy or nuanced social skills, which are critical in a digital company's team-based organization. Coaching can help. And on the whole, taking a risk on a younger person with expertise in the digital world, but who lacks experience running an organization, may be a better bet than turning to traditional leaders who lack the relevant cognition, skills, and psychology.

The digital giants are few in number. There are only about twenty worldwide. But their leaders, too, face competition. Many succeeded as a first mover in their space, with little to no competition. They now have to think about whether they can continue to grow on the path they've chosen, or whether to succumb to pressure to boost earnings per share at the risk of slower growth. Even with well-developed moneymaking models, platforms, brands, and consumer connections, new challenges are emerging, such as dealing with regulators or taming culture.

I feel confident that a new generation of leaders will arise to meet the challenges of today's digital world, probably from many different sources. Clarity about the criteria these leaders must meet will help identify them. Clearing a path for their growth will allow them to develop, probably much faster than we think. It may mean overlooking others to favor the necessary skills over extensive experience. Organizations that understand how digital leaders are different, and search them out and nurture them, will have an edge over companies that do not.

That's competitive advantage in the digital age.

CHAPTER 9

====

RETHINKING COMPETITIVE
ADVANTAGE IN THE REAL WORLD

Now that you understand the rules of competitive advantage that the digital giants so brilliantly discovered, your challenge is to use them. Most companies are starting not with a clean slate but with some considerable advantages that could be adapted to the digital age. Integrating the existing capabilities with digital technology and shedding what no longer works can unlock a path to 10x growth. I have seen leaders ponder this with their teams. When the combination clicks and a clear trajectory emerges, it releases tremendous energy.

Use the rules to work through all the changes that must occur—for example, in moneymaking, retraining and reorganizing people, and building a new ecosystem. The prize is seeing the elements, or building blocks, of competitive advantage combine and accelerate the transition to being reborn as a digital company.

At the time I started researching and writing this book, traditional companies that were becoming truly digital were rare exceptions. Now more companies, many of them in the business-to-business space, have begun to move. Honeywell, for example, is integrating its domain and digital expertise, augmented by a broader ecosystem, to become a provider of platforms to the life sciences industry. It did not create that market space but will greatly expand it while accelerating its own revenue growth.

At Aptiv, the part of Delphi that was spun off to focus on technology, executive chairman Raj Gupta and CEO Kevin Clark are driving the transformation of an old, declining auto parts supplier to be an expander of the mobility space. No longer just a maker of mechanical parts like power trains, it will supply computing platforms that use data from sensors and advanced software to support and expand the realm of autonomous vehicles.

Any outsider can see the major shifts that are afoot at some of our largest, most-established companies. Walmart, for example, is an easy one to watch because of its high visibility. It's been building its digital capability and at the same time turning what some consider a financial albatross into a competitive advantage: It is conceiving of its 3,571 "supercenters"—the large-footprint stores that include groceries as well as merchandise—as hubs for providing an expanding range of consumer experiences.

In September 2019, it opened its first-ever healthcare clinic in a Walmart store near Atlanta, Georgia. The prototype would allow the company to experiment and improve the concept. The idea is to give people a low-cost, accessible way to access preventative healthcare, including blood tests, X-rays, and eye exams. Given that 90 percent of the U.S. population is within ten miles of a Walmart store, and since people may be more inclined to use health services if they are already at the store to shop or pick up things they ordered online, the impact of the health clinics could be huge. Dentistry and veterinary care could follow, as could financial services and beauty. All of those things represent new sources of revenue based on using square footage Walmart already has.

The supercenter hubs would also be integral parts of Walmart's sprawling distribution system and house the computing capacity to drive the company's growing use of AI, machine learning, robotics, and other technology applications. That widely dispersed computing power located close to users, known as edge computing, speeds processing. Walmart CEO Doug McMillon says any extra capacity could be sold to other businesses, for example, to power autonomous vehicles, which depend on processing speed. So edge computing at the supercenter hubs could provide an additional source of revenues and profits while helping serve Walmart customers better.

While Walmart has been improving its e-commerce presence, in part by acquiring smaller digital start-ups like Bonobos and ModCloth, it has added third parties to its Marketplace site. Those third-party sellers can use Walmart's strengthening fulfillment services, and they are inclined to trust Walmart more than Amazon, which some see as having a conflict of interest. Walmart now offers seventy-five hundred brands, making Marketplace more competitive in the online space. As e-commerce grows, revenues rise, and margins do, too. The data that gets collected can be anonymized and sold to advertisers.

Changes in Walmart's social engine are also evident. The company acquired a lot of technology talent and a different mindset when it acquired Jet.com in 2016. In May 2019, it hired Suresh Kumar as chief technology officer and chief development officer. Kumar had worked at Microsoft, Google, and Amazon. And in October 2019, when John Furner was named president and CEO of Walmart U.S., McMillon remarked that Furner "is embracing new ways of working and thinking" and later added that Furner "thinks digitally."

Walmart has been redesigning jobs as it incorporates technology into everyday work and focuses on the customer experience. It established two hundred academies to retrain hundreds of thousands of employees in soft skills, such as how to be a good coach, as well as hard skills related to their newly redefined jobs. McMillon has tried to expand their sense of purpose to go beyond Walmart founder Sam Walton's famous words from 1992, shortly before he passed away: "We have a purpose, and the purpose is we save people money and help them live a better life." McMillon has added that it's more than price. It's value, ease of use, and fun.

McMillon's background as a hard-nosed traditional business leader who spent most of his career in merchandising jobs at Walmart has not prevented him from reinventing Walmart's competitive advantage. He has conceived of multiple ways that a combination of technology and existing physical space can give customers things they need and want. And while he is convinced that there is an important role for stores to play, he reverts to the customer's perspective. "If customers don't want stores, we won't have stores," he told Karen Short, an analyst at Barclays Capital, in December 2019. CFO Brett Biggs adds: "The way we look at it is we've got to go where the customer wants to go."

While McMillon and his team seem to have great clarity and conviction, they have to grapple with the financial challenges of executing the vision. Even if they see a path to 10x or 20x growth, can they manage the operating income to get there? Biggs says, "It's the job of management to make it work financially." The costly acquisitions of Jet.com and Flipkart in India meant increasing losses from e-commerce, Biggs notes, but investments they had made years before in productivity and other things inside the U.S. stores had started to pay back.

As Walmart manages the pace of its transformation to a digital company, McMillon is convinced that the pieces will work together, and for the sake of the customer. Investments are viewed on that basis—not as discrete initiatives but for how they look from a customer standpoint and in total.

By figuring out how to leverage a physical hub and combine it with the power of technology, McMillon may have found a new source of competitive advantage. Walmart will likely expand the market at first, then give Amazon a run for its money. It may prove to be easier for Walmart to install the technology than for Amazon to create hubs like Walmart's. Walmart doesn't lack financial resources, and it may also have an edge in its human touch with customers as opposed to Amazon's metrics-driven culture. So the tables may turn.

Human beings create change. New sources of competitive advantage will emerge, and the competitive landscape will shift. This is what drives human progress and our standard of living. You can be part of it.

ACKNOWLEDGMENTS

This book is the product of my learning through observation of and discussion with many thoughtful and accomplished business leaders. I am especially grateful for the generosity of those who allowed me to see firsthand how they are boldly leading their companies into the digital age. In particular I wish to thank Kathy Murphy and Ram Subramanian; Jorge Paulo Lemann, Carlos Alberto Sicupira, Miguel Gutierrez, Anna Saicali, and Cecilia Sicupira; and Krishna Sudheendra and Paras Chandaria. Their openness has expanded my learning, and their experiences will surely give other leaders greater confidence to move forward.

I also want to thank the many leaders I have worked with over time, whose knowledge, experience, and insights continually deepen my understanding of business practice. These include Gautam Adani, Bob Beachaump, Kumar Birla, Larry Bossidy, Bob Bradway, James Broadhead, Bruce Broussard, Dick Brown, Mike Butler, Indu Chandaria, Albert Chao, James Chao, John Chao, Dorothy Chao, Bill Conaty, Lodewijk de Vink, Amrish Goel, David Goel,

Aaron Greenblatt, Raj Gupta, Fred Hassan, Rod Hochman, Chad Holliday, Tim Huval, Andre Gerdau Johannpeter, John Koster, Jack Krol, Dejian Liu, Aloke Lohia, Suchitra Lohia, Alex Mandl, Harsh Mariwala, Melinda Merino, Brian Moynihan, Jac Nasser, Marc Onetto, Sajan Pillai, Vincent Roche, Ivan Seidenberg, Kirit Shah, Jim Shanley, Bhavna Shivpuri, Ling Tang, Ed Woolard, Tadashi Yanai, Julia Yang, Qian Ying, Qin Yingling, and the late great Jack Welch.

Monish Kumar of BCG, John MacCormick of Dickinson College, and Doug Peterson of S&P Global made important contributions to the book. I greatly respect their expertise and am deeply grateful for their time and help.

I am also grateful to Roger Scholl and Paul Whitlatch, two editors whose enthusiasm and skillful editorial support helped bring this book to fruition. Roger recognized the need in the business community and helped conceptualize the book, while Paul provided incisive editorial advice as he guided it to its final form. Thank you to Katie Berry and the production and marketing teams at Currency for their careful shepherding and support. And to John Mahaney, my editor of many previous books, whose teaching about writing and editing endures.

I want to pay a special tribute to my co-author, Geri Willigan, who has been with me for twenty-seven years as a partner in developing intellectual content and capturing it in writing. She and I brainstorm ideas almost daily as we seek new insights that will help leaders improve their companies. Her contribution to researching and writing this book was invaluable.

I am as always grateful to my longtime business partner, John Joyce, whose inputs and perspective are tremendously helpful, and to Jon Galli.

And I am grateful for the intelligence, competence, and care with which my assistants Cynthia Burr and Lisa Laubert support my work on a daily basis. They make it possible for me to sustain my work and accomplish projects like this.

Last, I am grateful to the community of business thinkers and leaders who constantly search to deepen their knowledge, improve their organizations, and make the world a better place for all.

ARE YOU READY TO BUILD COMPETITIVE ADVANTAGE IN THE DIGITAL AGE?

The following questions may help you think through how to create competitive advantage in the digital age, and whether you are truly up for it. The more you apply imagination, practicality, and intellectual honesty in answering them, the more helpful they will be.

1. Are you driven to improve the end-to-end customer experience and new ways to shape an ecosystem around an evolving set of algorithms and AI? This is not a game you can delegate. Is your personal psychology geared for it? Do you have the imagination to envision what the business will be and the grit, resilience, perseverance, and energy to drive it? Many leaders have not experienced this pace, this kind of nonlinear growth, which does not show a return on investment for years. Be honest about whether you are psychologically suited to the pace and the degree of risk.

2. What is your vision of a customer experience or need that could be a 10x or 100x demand space? What part of that space will you participate in? Are you focused squarely on the consumer experience or constantly comparing yourself against the competition? Make your observations of the consumer and map the touchpoints in the end-to-end experience today and in the future. This vision can be informed by data analytics and knowledge of emerging technologies, but use your judgment. Don't start by thinking about the assets you have and pondering how to deploy them. And don't limit your thinking because of barriers you assume exist. Think: What is needed? What don't we have? Narrate that vision for others to grasp.

3. What is the digital platform you need and how will it connect with the ecosystem? Its design must allow for agility, daily improvement, dynamic pricing, and so on. This question must be answered by a team that blends technical digital experts with nontechnical domain experts. Answering this and the previous question is likely to be iterative. What will data and algorithms allow you to get progressively better at?

4. How will moneymaking work? Do you subscribe to a moneymaking model that allows you to innovate continuously for the customer, offering lower prices and at the same time creating shareholder value? Does your model reflect the law of increasing returns and the generation of cash gross margin?

5. Who are your funders? In most cases you will need a series of funding. Incumbents will do everything to prevent you from gaining a foothold—legally via dynamic pricing or by brushing up against the legal antitrust line and settling later (think Microsoft's dominance of computer operating systems). Some funders will plan and invest a ton of money to get penetration to the right level; they see it as an investment, not an expense (Reliance "invested" in e-commerce by offering free mobile service).

6. What kinds of people and leaders do you need to make it happen? How will they work together? Will teams be co-located and focused on one task that is linked to the overall consumer-related mission? Where can you reduce most decisions to one level of approval? Do you have the digital platform to support transparency across the organization?

7. What is the feedback loop that will allow you to continuously experiment, learn, and improve the existing vision of the end-to-end customer experience or to imagine a new vision of a customer experience? By allowing continuous experimenting and learning, algorithms and AI make strategy dynamic, not fixed. This is what can drive exponential expansion, especially by creating new streams of revenue.

Even as you map out the next steps for your strategic initiative and assign the teams, stay focused on the consumer and abreast of what technology can do *now*. Keep the data flowing, search for insights, and stimulate your creative thinking. Then cycle through the questions again. That's how you'll keep your competitive edge sharp and your business relevant for the long term.

NOTES

CHAPTER 1: WHY THE DIGITAL GIANTS ARE WINNING

7   **The news prompted media analyst:** Alex Sherman, "How the Epic 'Lord of the Rings' Deal Explains Amazon's Slow-Burning Media Strategy," CNBC.com, March 8, 2019, https://www.cnbc.com/2019/03/08/amazon-prime-video-feature.html.

CHAPTER 3: MARKET SPACES OF 10X, 100X, 1000X

39   **"When given the choice":** Brad Stone, *The Everything Store: Jeff Bezos and the Age of Amazon* (New York: Little, Brown, 2013), 273.

39   **As far back as the 1990s:** Ibid., 41.

41   **"Everything we do in technology":** Microsoft website, https://news.microsoft.com/transform/starbucks-turns-to-technology-to-brew-up-a-more-personal-connection-with-its-customers.

53   **Revenue from e-commerce in India:** India Brand Equity Foundation, "E-commerce Industry in India,"

updated January 2020, https://www.ibef.org/industry/ecommerce.aspx.

CHAPTER 4: DIGITAL PLATFORMS AT THE CENTER OF THE BUSINESS

60 **PageRank made it possible:** An excellent source for a nontechnical explanation of PageRank and other basic algorithms is John MacCormick, *Nine Algorithms That Changed the Future: The Ingenious Ideas That Drive Today's Computers* (Princeton, N.J.: Princeton University Press, 2012).

61 **Google believes the new sequence:** Rob Copeland, "Google Lifts Veil, a Little, into Secretive Search Algorithm Changes," *The Wall Street Journal,* October 25, 2019.

61 **So he asked a handful:** Brad Stone, *The Everything Store: Jeff Bezos and the Age of Amazon* (New York: Little, Brown, 2013), 51.

61 **"the seed that would grow":** Ibid.

62 **Walmart had dabbled:** Per Internet Retailer via Applico.

62 **In 2018, although still:** Sarah Perez, "Walmart Passes Apple to Become No. 3 Online Retailer in U.S.," *TechCrunch,* November 16, 2018.

68 **DaaS—Disney as a service:** Matthew Ball, "Disney as a Service: Why Disney Is Closer Than Ever to Walt's 60 Year Old Vision," *REDEF ORIGINAL,* May 10, 2016.

69 **That arrangement preserves:** "Gartner Says Worldwide IaaS Public Cloud Services Market Grew 31.3% in 2018," Gartner, Inc., press release, Stamford, Conn., July 29, 2019.

70 **"the commonality in data":** Arthur Yeung and Dave

Ulrich, *Reinventing the Organization* (Boston: Harvard Business Review Press, 2019), 104.

73 **That concept was the basis:** Ming Zeng, "Alibaba and the Future of Business," *Harvard Business Review,* September–October 2018.

CHAPTER 5: VALUE-CREATING ECOSYSTEMS

84 **Honeywell and Bigfinite:** "Honeywell, Bigfinite Collaborate to Drive Digital Transformation," Contractpharma.com, February 2, 2020.

86 **"Goldman Sachs has begun":** Laura Noonan, "Goldman Sachs in Talks with Amazon to Offer Small Business Loans," *Financial Times,* February 3, 2020.

99 **As reported by Reuters:** Heather Somerville and Paul Lienert, "Inside SoftBank's Push to Rule the Road," Reuters, April 13, 2019.

100 **Apple is now shaping:** Morgan Stanley's research report, *Apple, Inc., Don't Underestimate Apple's Move into Healthcare,* April 8, 2019, is the source for much of the specific data used throughout this section.

103 **Divya Nag:** Maya Ajmera, "Conversations with Maya: Divya Nag," *Science News,* September 13, 2018.

CHAPTER 6: MONEYMAKING FOR DIGITALS

116 **"There are suddenly becoming":** Ian Thibodeau, "Delphi to Split into Aptiv and Delphi Tech," *The Detroit News,* September 27, 2017.

118 **A headline in *The New York Times*:** Karen Weise, "Amazon's Profit Falls Sharply as Company Buys Growth," *The New York Times,* October 24, 2019.

126 **As CEO Reed Hastings said:** Alex Sherman, "Netflix

CEO Reed Hastings Says Subscriber Numbers Aren't the Right Metric to Track Competition," CNBC.com, November 6, 2019.

127   **It chooses companies:** Liza Lin and Julie Steinberg, "How China's Tencent Uses Deals to Crowd Out Tech Rivals," *The Wall Street Journal*, May 15, 2018.

CHAPTER 7: TEAMS INSTEAD OF ORGANIZATIONAL LAYERS

133   **What matters is embracing:** For more on Amazon's internal operations, see my book (co-authored with Julia Yang), *The Amazon Management System: The Ultimate Digital Business Engine That Creates Extraordinary Value for Both Customers and Shareholders* (Washington, D.C.: Ideapress Publishing, 2019).

151   **"As the team worked":** Ron Miller, "How AWS Came to Be," *TechCrunch,* July 2, 2016, https://techcrunch.com/2016/07/02/andy-jassys-brief-history-of-the-genesis-of-aws/.

CHAPTER 9: RETHINKING COMPETITIVE ADVANTAGE IN THE REAL WORLD

179   **"If customers don't want":** FactSet CallStreet transcript of Walmart, Inc., Barclays Gaming, Lodging, Leisure, Restaurant & Food Retail Conference, December 4, 2019.

179   **CFO Brett Biggs adds:** FactSet CallStreet transcript of Walmart, Inc., UBS Global Consumer & Retail Conference, March 5, 2020.

179   **Biggs says, "It's the job":** Ibid.

INDEX

Acrobat Reader, 67
Admatic, 80
Adobe Systems, 47, 67, 116, 121
advertising, 37, 66, 74
Aetna, 65, 104
AgileCraft, 144
agile development, 141–45, 154
Airbnb, 19, 25, 64, 109
Algorithmia, 61
algorithms, xiii, xvii, 4, 5, 10, 14–16, 21, 30, 32, 33, 46, 48, 53–55, 57–62, 65–67, 70–75, 89, 102, 104, 107, 114, 119, 120, 131, 166, 173, 185–87
Alibaba, xiii, 9, 25, 32, 52, 54–55, 57, 58, 68–71, 73, 84, 97–99, 106, 110, 116, 126

Alipay, 55, 69
AlliedSignal, 152
Alphabet, 39, 102
Amazon, xiii–xiv, xvi, 6–9, 11, 12, 15–16, 19, 23, 25, 26, 29, 32–34, 38–39, 47, 49–50, 52, 55, 56, 58, 61, 62, 66, 69, 72, 75–76, 81, 97, 102, 105, 107, 109, 111–13, 116, 119, 121, 122, 126, 129–31, 141, 143, 152, 172, 177–80
Amazon Alexa, 84, 86, 122
Amazon Lending, 86
Amazon Marketplace, 65, 68, 85, 86, 141
Amazon Web Services (AWS), 8, 68, 119, 122, 150, 151
Ame, 81
Americanas.com, 76–77
Amgen, 102

Android, 93
Ant Financial, 69, 73
Apollo, 93
Apple, xvi, 6, 7, 11, 15–16,
  26, 40, 43, 46, 51, 72–75,
  83, 100–105, 113, 122,
  124–26, 131
Apple HealthKit, 103
Apple Pay, 8
Apple ResearchKit, 103
AppleTV+, 125
Apple Watch, 72, 100, 103–4
Aptiv, 115, 176
Arm Holdings, 91, 98
Arthur, W. Brian, 11n
artificial intelligence, 10,
  36, 40, 48, 53, 59, 61, 63,
  71, 81, 93, 166, 177, 185,
  187
AT&T Company, xvii, 6
Audi, 84, 92
automobile industry, 22–25,
  30, 87–93, 99, 169–70
autonomous (self-driving)
  vehicles (AVs), 88–89, 92,
  93, 169, 177
Away, 50–51, 56

B2W, 9, 15, 32, 34, 76–81,
  116, 164, 173
B2W Marketplace, 79
BAIC, 93
Baidu, 93, 97

Bain & Company, 25
Ball, Matthew, 68
BAMTech, 161, 162
Bank of America, 57
bankruptcy, 20
Barnes & Noble, 49
Bayes, Thomas, 59
Bayes' theorem, 59
BERT (Bidirectional Encoder
  Representations from
  Transformers), 61
Best Buy, 8, 35
Bezos, Jeff, xiii–xiv, 23, 33,
  38, 39, 49, 61, 85, 97, 111,
  113, 114, 116, 118, 133,
  141, 150, 152
Big Bazaar hypermarket
  chain, 44
Bigfinite, 84–85
Biggs, Brett, 179
Biyani, Kishore, 43–44
Blockbuster, 4, 6
BMW, 84, 87, 92, 170
Bock, Laszlo, 152
Bombas, 50
Bonobos, 177
Bossidy, Larry, 152
Boston Consulting Group
  (BCG), 25, 27, 40, 146
boundaries, acceptance of
  existing, 28–30
brand, 22, 25, 37
Brazil, 9, 34, 52, 75–81

Brigham and Women's
  Hospital, 105
Brin, Sergey, xiii, 60, 151, 159
broadband technology, 4,
  5, 13
business plans, 28

Cainiao, 70–71, 84
Cambridge Analytica, 75
capital expenditures (capex),
  117, 118
capital investment, 22
cash, 13, 22, 108–17, 121–25,
  128
cash cows, 27
Casper, 50–51, 56
Chapek, Bob, 170
China, 29, 34, 64, 67, 89,
  92–93, 99, 123, 127
Chrysler Corporation, 23
churn rate, 120–21
Clark, Kevin, 176
Coca-Cola, 28
Comcast, 5
Competitive Advantage
  (Porter), 24
Competitive Strategy
  (Porter), 24
computer industry, 31–32, 36,
  83, 113
consumer experience and
  preferences, 16, 17, 28–45,
  47, 49, 50, 54, 55, 64, 66,

101, 111, 121, 134, 137–40,
  185–87
consumer privacy, 74–75, 100,
  101
Cook, Tim, 7, 72, 101
Copeland, Rob, 60–61
core competencies, 26, 33, 35,
  44–45
coronavirus pandemic, xv,
  xvi, 56, 124
cost structure, 37, 108, 119
courage, leadership and,
  167–68
Cramer, Jim, 101
Crone, Nathan, 104
Cruise Automation, 88,
  93–94, 98, 99
culture, 153

Daimler, 92, 93, 170
data breaches, 74
DBS Bank, 57–58
decision-making, 12
Delphi Technologies, 115–16,
  176
department store chains, 56
De Vos, Glen, 116
Didi Chuxing, 34, 64, 67, 89,
  92, 93, 99, 123
digital platforms, 54–82, 186
diminishing returns, 12
Disney+, 7, 50, 51, 62, 124,
  126, 161, 162, 164, 170

Disney Company, xvi, xvii, 6, 7, 15–16, 26, 27, 50, 51, 56, 62, 68, 124, 126, 160–63, 168, 170, 171, 173

distribution systems, 23–25, 33, 35, 37

dogs, 27

Dollar Shave Club, 8

DRAMs (dynamic random access memory chips), 51

DVDs, 4, 5

dynamic pricing, 64–65, 186

earnings per share (EPS), 13, 27, 108, 111, 114, 118, 121, 124, 127, 128, 162

eBay, 69

ecosystems, 11, 13, 14, 21, 29, 50, 55, 70, 72, 111, 169, 175, 176, 185, 186

value-creating, 83–107

edge computing, 177

electric cars, 87–88

emergent leadership, 152

encryption technology, 75

end-to-end consumer experience, 36–38, 41–43, 47, 49, 50, 54, 55, 64, 101, 137, 185, 187

E-smart, 80

Euromoney, 58

European Union, 75

Everything Store, The (Stone), 61

Execution (Charan and Bossidy), 152

expense ratio, 119–20

exponential growth, 13, 31–35, 37, 55, 66, 112, 129

Facebook, xiii, 8, 39, 75, 126, 143

facial recognition, 75

Fast Retailing, 43

Fidelity Personal Investing, xv, 15, 42, 75, 130–31, 133–49, 151, 153–57, 164, 172

Fidelity Wealth Management, 120

Fidelity ZERO, 140–41

Financial Times, 86–87

first mover advantage, 9

Flipkart, 9, 34, 51, 52, 98, 110, 179

Food and Drug Administration (FDA), 104

Ford Motor Company, 23, 25, 30, 87, 91, 169–70

fraud detection, 60, 64

funding and funders, 108–10, 126–28, 187

Furner, John, 178

Future Group, 43–44

G&A (general and administrative) costs, 117, 119
Garmin, 102
Gartner, Inc., 69
Gates, Bill, 22, 31–32, 151
General Electric, 29, 64, 71–72
General Motors, 23, 25, 30, 88, 91, 93–94, 98, 99
Global Finance, 58
Goldman Sachs, 86–87
Google, xiii–xiv, 8, 39, 58, 60–61, 63–64, 68, 74, 116, 126, 138, 143, 151–52, 178
Google Gmail, 63
Google Maps, 63–64
Google Open Source, 64
Google Search, 60, 63
Grab, 99
Greenblatt, Robert, 6
Greenfield, Rich, 7
gross margin, 13, 22, 47, 108, 111–15, 119, 122–24, 186
Gupta, Piyush, 57–58
Gupta, Raj, 176
Gutierrez, Miguel, 77

hacking, 74
Hamel, Gary, 25, 44

Harry's razors, 50–51, 56
Harvard University, 80
Hastings, Reed, xvi, 4–5, 13–15, 27, 114, 125, 126, 170
HBO, 6, 7, 51
HBO Max, xvii, 125
HBO Now, 161
Health app (Apple), 72–73, 103
healthcare ecosystem, 72, 74–75, 100–105
health insurance, 66–67
Hertz, 26
Honda, 84, 93, 99
Honeywell, 84–85, 152, 176
horizontal integration, 46
hotel industry, 25
Hulu, 5, 7, 26, 56, 124, 161, 162, 168

IBM Corporation, 68, 105
Ideais, 80
Iger, Bob, 124, 160–64, 168, 170
Inc. magazine, 4
increasing returns, 11, 17, 21, 108, 112, 186
incrementalism, 25–27, 45
India, 9, 10, 34, 44, 46–47, 51–53, 58–59, 75, 94, 162, 179

initial public offering (IPO),
    110
Instagram, 24
Intel, 83–84, 93
internal rate of return (IRR),
    117
Internet, 32, 33, 39, 41, 47,
    51, 54, 57, 60
investment banking, 46,
    110
iPhone, 83, 100, 103, 131
iPod, 100

J. Crew, 20
Jassy, Andy, 68, 150–51
JCPenney, 20, 56
JD.com, 9, 32
Jet.com, 9, 26, 56, 62, 178,
    179
Jio, 47, 51–52
JioMart, 34, 52
Jira Align, 144
Jobs, Steve, 22, 43, 113, 151,
    161
Justice Department, U.S.
    Department of, 6

Kimberley-Clark, 23
Kindle, 122
Knauss, Gregory, 104
KPN, 29
Kumar, Monish, 146
Kumar, Suresh, 178

Lafley, A. G., 46
leadership, 12–13, 21, 30,
    147–49, 152, 156, 158,
    159–74, 185, 187
legacy companies, 8, 15, 16,
    41, 43, 45, 48, 55, 56, 73,
    97, 114–15, 124, 134–35,
    157, 166, 171, 172
Lenovo, 64
Levitt, Ted, 89
Li, Robin, 97
licensing fees, 14
LinkedIn, 64
liquidity trap, 114, 115
loans, 66
Lojas Americanas, 34,
    75–78, 81
Lore, Marc, 62
Lowy, Frank, 126–27, 160
Lucasfilm Ltd., 161
Lyft, 19, 25, 34, 64, 67, 84, 92,
    123

Ma, Jack, 54–55, 97, 106
MacCormick, John, 60
machine learning, 10, 53, 59,
    60, 71, 74, 100, 177
Macy's, 8, 56
Mahindra, 91
market segments, 30, 35, 39
market share, 27, 37, 127
market space, 35, 46, 50–53
Martin-Flickinger, Gerri, 41

Marvel Entertainment, 161
Massachusetts Institute of
    Technology (MIT), 61, 80,
    95–96, 156
mass production and
    markets, 30, 37
matrix reporting structures,
    132
Mayer, Kevin, 162
Mayo Clinic, 105
MBA programs, 25
McKinsey & Company,
    25, 46
McMillon, Doug, 26, 52, 62,
    159, 177–79
Mercedes, 92
Microsoft, 8, 36–37, 47, 68,
    83–84, 93, 105, 143, 159,
    178, 187
Miller, Ron, 150–51
minimum viable product
    (MVP), 130, 166–67
Mitsubishi, 88
mixed reality, 36
mobile phones, 32, 47, 52,
    83, 113
Mobileye, 88
ModCloth, 177
Monet Technologies, 99
moneymaking, 108–28,
    186
Mubadala Investment
    Company, 109

Murdoch, Rupert, 160, 162
Murphy, Kathy, 130, 133–35,
    137–40, 142, 143, 146–49,
    153, 155, 156, 164
Musk, Elon, 87–88

Nadella, Satya, 36, 159
Nag, Divya, 103
NBC, xvi, 5
NBCUniversal, xvii, 11,
    125
Neiman Marcus, 20
Netflix, xvi–xvii, 3–8, 10,
    11, 13–16, 19, 26, 27, 29,
    39, 46, 47, 51, 62, 111,
    113, 121, 125, 126, 138,
    153, 160, 170–71
New York Times, The, 118,
    126
Nike, 26
Nissan, 88
Nokia, 92
Noonan, Laura, 86–87
Nordstrom, 127
Nvidia, 91
NYU Langone Medical
    Center, 104

observational acumen,
    43–45, 166
Ola, 99
OneMarket, 127
Opel, 91

operating expenses (opex),
117, 118
organizational layers,
129–132, 140–43, 154, 156
outdated theories,
overreliance on, 24–27

P.C. Richard, 35
Page, Larry, xiii, 60, 151, 159
PageRank, 60
Pantaloons, 44
patents, 22, 25
PayPal, 8, 64
Peacock, 125
Pepsi, 28
personalized consumer
experience, 21, 39–41,
61, 66
Peugeot, 88
PillPack, 65
Pixar, 160–61
Porter, Michael, 24, 25
Prahalad, C. K., 24–25, 44
price gap, 48–49
privacy, 74–75, 100, 101
Procter & Gamble, 8, 23, 46,
171
proprietary technology, 22

Qantas Airlines, 66–67
quantum computing, 36
question marks, 27

Rakuten, 32
Reinventing the Organization
(Yeung and Ulrich), 69–70
Reliance Industries, 34, 51,
53, 187
Renault, 84
return on investment (ROI),
117
Reuters, 99
revenue, 20, 22, 108, 111, 112,
115, 119–24
ride-sharing companies, 11,
19, 24, 25, 34, 64, 67, 84,
89–92, 98, 99, 109, 110,
113, 119, 122–24
Ryan, Matt, 40

Saicali, Anna, 77–81, 164
Samsung, 102
Sauer, Patrick J., 5
scale of distribution, 23
Schindler, 72
Schmidt, Eric, 151
scrum masters, 144–45
Sequoia, 110
Shopify, 56, 63
ShopRunner, 71
Shoptime, 77
Short, Karen, 179
short-term thinking, 27
Sicupira, Carlos Alberto, 77
Similarities, 61

simultaneous dialogue,
130–31, 156–57

Slack, 110

social engines, 21, 129, 150,
151, 156, 178

social media, 24, 29, 37

SoftBank Group, 93, 98–99

Vision Fund, 52, 98,
109–10

Sold by Amazon, 65

Son, Masayoshi, 98–100, 109

speech recognition, 60

Spielberg, Steven, 3, 7

Spotify, 24

Stanford University, 80, 96,
104

Starbucks, 40–41

stars, 27

steel industry, 22–23

Stem Cell Theranostics, 103

Stone, Brad, 61

Submarino, 76, 77

Subramanian, Ram, 143, 148,
156

Sudheendra, Krishna, 57

SWOT analysis, 28

Taobao, 69

Target, 51

Tarkena, 80

teams, 12, 130–33, 135–36,
140–49, 151, 154–57, 187

TechCrunch, 150–51

Tencent, 9, 29, 32, 58, 110, 127

TensorFlow, 63–64

terms-of-service
agreements, 74

Tesla, 87–88

Theory brand, 43

third-party sellers, 11, 65, 66,
79, 111, 141

Tiger Fund, 110

Tiger Global, 79

Time Warner, 6

Tmall, 55, 69, 84

Tmall Genie, 84

Tmall Genie Auto, 84

Tmall Global, 69

Toyota, 87, 99

traditional companies, 4, 12,
14, 16, 17, 19–20, 26, 29,
30, 33–34, 62–63, 117, 132,
133, 153, 157, 172, 175

Turner Broadcasting, 6

TuSimple, 89

23andMe, 103

Twenty-First Century Fox, 7,
16, 27, 160, 162, 168

Twitter, 7, 39

Uber, 11, 19, 24, 25, 34, 64,
67, 92, 98, 99, 109, 110,
113, 119, 122–24

Ulrich, Dave, 69

Unibail-Rodamco SE, 126–27
Uniconsult, 80
unicorn status, 98
Unilever, 23
Uniqlo brand, 43
UnitedHealth, 104
UPS (United Parcel
Service), 89
UST, 94–97

Vauxhall, 91
Verizon, 126, 164
vertical integration, 46
VHS tapes, 5
video streaming, xvi–xvii,
3–8, 10, 11, 13–16, 19,
26–27, 29, 50, 51, 62, 121,
124–26, 160–62, 168,
170–71
Volkswagen, 93
Volvo, 84

Wall Street Journal, The,
60–61
Walmart, xvi, 8, 9, 26,
32, 34, 41, 50–52, 56,

62, 81, 110, 113, 119, 159,
176–80
Walmart.com, 62
Walton, Sam, 41, 178
WarnerMedia, xvi, 6, 11,
15–16, 26, 51, 125
Waymo, 88, 92
WeChat, 29
Weibo, 84
Westfield Corporation, 126,
160
WeWork, 98, 110
Wilke, Jeff, 130, 152
winner takes all
generalization, 9
Wiseman, Liz, 147
Worldwide Consumer, 130,
152

Yanai, Tadashi, 43
Yeung, Arthur, 69
YouTube, 5

Zook, Chris, 44
Zuckerberg, Mark, xiii, 22,
75, 159

ABOUT THE AUTHOR

My mission:

- To help business practitioners become better.

What I do:

- A sounding board, problem solver, and builder of trusted relationships over long periods of time with CEOs, boards, and other executives across the globe.
- Board self-evaluations and candid feedback to improve board practice.
- Facilitate board-management relationships.
- Twenty-nine books, four bestsellers, all geared for practitioners based on observation on the ground.
- Help select great leaders and board members.
- Help companies digitize, change their business models, and create three-layer organizations.
- Has served on a dozen boards in the United States, Canada, Brazil, India, and China. Currently active on five boards.
- MBA with high distinction and DBA from Harvard Business School. Best teacher awards. Distinguished Fellow of the National Association of Human Resources.

Ram-Charan.com

Available from #1 *New York Times* bestselling author

RAM CHARAN

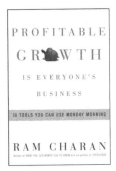

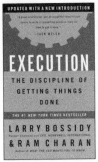

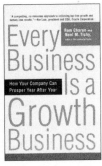

"Ram Charan is the most influential consultant alive."

—*Fortune*

"Charan has an unparalleled track record of providing executives with compelling yet practical advice on how to succeed in tumultuous business environments."

—**IVAN G. SEIDENBERG, former chairman and CEO of Verizon**

CURRENCY

Available wherever books are sold